Gentlemen of Fortune

DERRICK KNIGHT

Gentlemen of Fortune

The Men who made their Fortunes
in Britain's Slave Colonies

Frederick Muller Limited
London

First published in Great Britain 1978 by
Frederick Muller Limited, London NW2 6LE

Copyright © 1978 Derrick Knight

ISBN 0 584 10165 1

British Library Cataloguing in Publication Data

Knight, Derrick
  Gentlemen of fortune.
  1. England — Social life and customs — 18th century
  2. West Indies — Social life and customs   3. West
  Indies — Colonization
  I. Title
  942.07'2   DA498

ISBN 0-584-10165-1

Printed by Biddles Ltd., Guildford, Surrey

For Brenda

Contents

List of Illustrations

Between pages 80-81

Acknowledgements

I wish to thank Martin Secker and Warburg Ltd for permission to use a passage from BOUND TO VIOLENCE by Yambo Ouologuem, translated by Ralph Manheim, the British Museum Print Room, the Guildhall Library, the Mary Evans Picture Library and the National Trust for permission to reproduce pictures in their collections and the British Museum Coins and Medals Department for permission to reproduce a Golden Guinea in their collection on the title page.

Introduction

The North London Primary School at the bottom of my road is
called the Beckford Junior School. Built in the reformist Victorian
seventies, it was named after a famous 18th century Lord Mayor,
friend of William Pitt and one of the richest city merchants whose
money came from his sugar plantations and slave trading in the
West Indies. It is unfair to suggest in our more enlightened century
that those earnest 19th century educationalists, bringing the three
R's to the deserving poor of the London suburbs, should have
been more sensitive to the record of such a man and his family
connections. But is it not ironical, at the very least, that the school
today echoes to the exuberant voices of children whose ancestors
were shipped in chains from the Guinea coast to Jamaica. I would
be prepared to bet that not a child or a teacher either has given the
matter a moment's thought. It was all such a long time ago and
surely it doesn't matter any more.

But it should, and does. The British Caribbean colonial
experience lasted over three hundred years. During the 18th
century the Caribbean islands and the North American colonies
together formed a trading empire of immense power and importance to Britain. Every trade in the Kingdom was involved as one
18th century pamphleteer was at pains to point out.

> ". . . there is hardly a ship comes to us, but what is half loaden at least . . .
> with English commodities. Several score of Thousands are employed in
> England, in furnishing the Plantations with all sorts of Necessaries, and
> these must be supplied the while with Cloths and Victuals, which employs
> great numbers likewise. All which are paid, out of our Industry and
> Labour.
>
> "We have yearly from England an infinite Quantity of Iron Wares ready

wrought. Thousands of Dozens of Howes, and great numbers of Bills to cut our Canes, many Barrels of Nails; many Sets of Smiths, Carpenters, and Coopers Tools; all our Locks and Hinges; with Swords, Pistols, Carbines, Muskets and Fowling Pieces.

We have also from England all sorts of Tin-ware, Earthenware and Wooden ware; and all our Brass and Pewter. And many a Serve of Sope, many a Quoyle of Rope, and of Lead many a Fodder, do the Plantations take from England.

Even English Cloth is much worn amongst us; but we have of Stuff far greater quantities. From England come all the Hats we weare; and of Shoes, thousands of dozens yearly. The white Broad-cloth that we use for Strainers, comes also to a great deal of Money. Our very Negro Caps, of Woollen-yarn knit (of which we have yearly thousands of Dozens) may pass for a Manufacture.

How many Spinners, Knitters, and Weavers are kept at work here in England, to make all the Stockings we wear? Woollen Stockings for the ordinary People, Silk Stockings when we could go to the price, Worsted Stockings in abundance, and Thread Stockings without number.

The Bread we eat, is of English Flower; we take great Quantities of English Beer, and of English Cheese and Butter; we sit by the light of English Candles; and the Wine we drink, is bought for the most part with English Commodities.

Moreover we take yearly thousands of Barrels of Irish Beef; with the price whereof those people pay their Rents, to their Landlords that live and spend their Estates in England. . .

'Tis strange we should be thought to diminish the People of England, when we do so much increase the Employments."

The Groans of the Plantations

Almost every family will, if it looks, find its own historical link with the West Indies. If not in trade, in one of the armed forces, in merchant shipping, or more directly by having a cadet who sailed out to find his fortune. The West Indies experience is part of our heritage and whether we like it or not, slavery and the whole-hearted acceptance of slavery is also part of our heritage; and as soon as slavery had been abolished, the abandonment of West Indies sugar in favour of cheaper East Indian sugar by the British Government of the day, is also part of our heritage and so is the consequence; the bankruptcy of the British West Indian sugar industry and our cynical betrayal of the huge "free" black labour force who depended on it for some kind of livelihood.

By that time, the "gentlemen of fortune" had gone home, the greater number in the so-called "silver age" of West Indian prosperity, the time between the end of the Seven Years War in 1763 and the American War of Independence; the rest taking their compensation money for freed slaves in the 1830's. They were not the most admirable group of citizens in our island history, but for a time they were certainly one of the most powerful. They shimmer like passing comets across the 18th century social scene — the pop stars of their age, as selfish, as opinionated and as raffish. They put up their own memorials in the form of ostentatious town and country houses; they imposed themselves on a fashionable society by congregating in huge family groups at fashionable spas, and indulged in prodigious hospitality in the metropolis; they bought their way into the landed gentry; they controlled a powerful business lobby in the city of London, which was able to sway a Parliamentary vote on frequent occasions. Without making too close a parallel they formed a sort of Mafia — a closed society of interests with more than a hint of violence and a Godfather figure, like William Beckford or Simon Taylor.

Directly or indirectly, this group of planters, merchants, professional military and naval men, lawyers, doctors and privateers have had a lasting and visible effect on the look and quality of modern Britain.

On the visible level, not only are many of the great Georgian houses built on West Indian money, but there is a close connection between the dramatic city developments of Marylebone and Oxford Street in London, and the Georgian explosion of Bath with the aspirations and riches of the returning West Indians. On a more mundane level, we find that new exotic foods and fruits commonplace in the Caribbean are imported successfully having become permanently popular. Rum — the spirit of molasses became a widespread social drink and turtle soup the obligatory first course without which no self-respecting banquet in the 19th century could possibly have continued.

In the political arena particularly, the West Indians found the manipulation of power in the unreformed House of Commons particularly to their liking. In the days before rigid Party distinctions, even quite small pressure groups of M.P.s had a major influence on a vote. The West Indian planters discovered even before the end of the 17th century that having their own M.P.'s did more to advance their special interests than any number of pleas and petitions directly from the Caribbean islands. But even in the cynical mid-18th century, the activities of these West Indian gentlemen in rigging elections, hawking their votes in return for office or privileges and celebrating all the worst features of the unreformed Parliamentary system, tended in the end to be counterproductive. Their exuberant criminality did wonders to focus the ideas of reformists and hasten the acceptance of change.

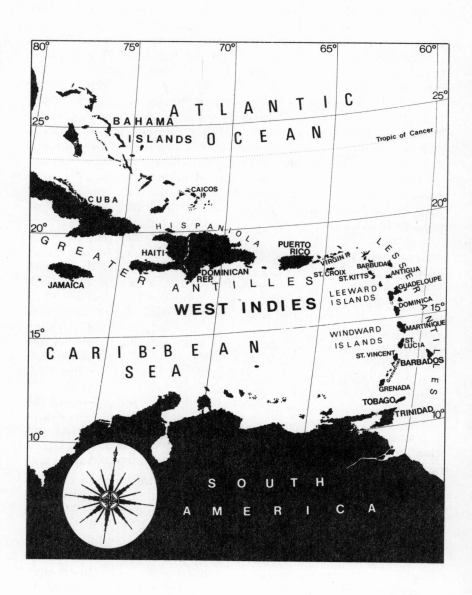

1

Prelude

In my school library, which had once belonged to an old Victorian gentleman, was a glowing shelf of large and beautifully tooled volumes published by the Hakluyt Society and called *The Principal Navigations, Voyages, Traffiques and Discoveries of the English Nation*. The volumes were kept strictly under lock and key and no-one had access to them until they were in the Sixth Form. Since the books were valuable, but not particularly old, the out of bounds rule gave them a mystery and appeal like a grown-up dirty book or 'X' Certificate movie, and even today, some thirty years later, I can remember the excitement of the first time I was allowed to handle the books and the quite extraordinary spell of reading the cool prose of everyday events of the 15th and 16th century exploration and conquest, told first hand by on the spot mariners and merchants. I had an insane desire to go rushing off to join the merchant navy there and then to seek my fortune at sea.

There too, as the pages turned, were the casual brutalities and horrors of everyday life with the great colonising pioneers. Death by fire and the gibbet, by drowning and disease, by starvation and thirst; the obsession with God and the passion for pounds, shillings and pence. Another world maybe, a far off time with other moralities and superstitions, but one which had chords of similarity with the 1940's through which we schoolboys were then living. The brutalities, the self-interest, the fascination with maps and campaigns, we knew them too; the appeal to a British sense of destiny and display of deeds of greatness sounded modern too.

But nowe it is high time for us to weight our ancre, to hoise up our sailes, to get cleare of these boistrous, frosty, and misty seas, and with all speede to direct our course for the milde, lightsome, temperate and warme

1

Atlantick Ocean, over which the Spaniards and Portugales have made so many pleasant prosperous and golden voyages. And albeit I cannot deny, that both of them in their East and West Indian Navigations have indured many tempests, dangers and shipwrecks: yet this dare I boldly affirme; first that a great number of them have satisfied their fame — thirsty and gold-thirsty mindes with that reputation and wealth, which made all perils and misadventure seeme tolerable unto them; and secondly, that their first attempts (which in this comparison I doe only stand upon) were no whit more difficult and dangerous, than ours to the Northeast.

"For admit that the way was much longer, yet was it never barred with yce, mist or darkness, but was at all seasons of the yeare open and navigable; yea and that for the most part with fortunate and fit gales of winde. Moreover they had no forren prince to intercept or molest them, but their owne Townes, Islands, and maine lands to succour them. The Spaniards had the Canary Isles: and so had the portugales the Isles of the Azores, of Porto Santo, of Madera, of Cape verd, the castle of Mina, the fruitfull and profitable Isle of St. Thomas, being all of them conveniently situated, and well fraught with commodities. And had they not continuall and yerely trade in some one part or other of Africa, for getting of slaves for sugar, for elephants' teeth, graines, silver, gold and other precious wares, which served as allurements to draw them on by little and little, and as proppes to stay them from giving over their attempts!"

And as one dipped in and out of the many volumes of *The Principal Navigations* so lovingly collected and annotated with translations from Anglo Saxon, Spanish and Portuguese texts, with its letters, diaries, bills of account, summaries of laws, maps and sketches, I realised that what these books were doing was to lay down a most convincing barrage of historical sources and texts to prove a case. The case that England had always been a country of backbone and enterprise and that she should make an even greater effort now with her seadogs and Spaniards on the run to make herself an Empire.

I was strongly reminded of this when researching the early history of our West Indian colonies. What or who made the hit-and-run raiders of the Elizabethan golden age come ashore and stay ashore? And part of the unavoidable answer was Richard Hakluyt, a man who never travelled further than France in his whole life, and yet has as much claim to be a founder of the British Empire as Captain Cook or Cecil Rhodes.

Despite his achievements, Richard Hakluyt remains a tantalising figure in the shadows of Elizabethan history. No portrait of him has ever been found. Born about 1553, five years before the first Queen Elizabeth came to the throne, he was educated to be a clergyman at Westminster and Oxford, and early on seems to have determined the course of his life, learning as many languages as he could and starting to collect his material.

2

Prelude

"... I grew familiarly acquainted with the chiefest Captaines at sea, the greatest Merchants, and the best Mariners of our nation: by which meanes having gotten somewhat more their common knowledge, I passed at length the narrow seas into France with Sir Edward Stafford, her Majesties carefull and discreet Ligier, where during my five yeeres abroad with him in his dangerous and chargeable residencie in her Highnes service, I both heard in speech, and read in books other nations miraculously extolled for their discoveries and notable enterprises by sea, but the English of all others for their sluggish security, and continuall neglect of the like attempts especially in so long and happy a time of peace, either ignominiously reported, or exceedingly condemned. . ."

His Epistle of dedication to Sir Francis Walsingham

Almost all we know about the man is from his own writing, the prefaces and dedications to the various editions of *The Navigations*. He makes his intentions clear.

I have in the first place exposed and set foorth to the view of this age with the same intention that the old Romans set up in wax in their places the Statues or images of their worthy ancestors . . . that by the remembring of their worthy actes, that flame was kindled in their noble breasts, and could never be quenched, untill such time as their owne valure had equalled the fame and glory of their progenitors. So though not in wax, yet in record of writing have I presented to the noble courages of this English Monarchie, the like images of their famous predecessors, with hope of like effect in their posteritie."

and goes on to advocate the English settlement of mainland America; to provide an argument for English merchants to muscle in on the Portuguese African trade, including slaves, because the most uptodate reports in his hands show them to be in a weak state. He also provides strong suggestive arguments for the opening up of new Far Eastern markets in Japan and Northern China where the cold seasons must make the people particularly disposed to buy good English woollens. Hakluyt is always practical. He gets hold of documents captured from Spanish galleons and from ports sacked by English expeditions and

"having gotten, to translate out of Spanish, and here in this present volume to publish such secrets of theirs as may in any way availe us and annoy them . . . most of all their secrets of the West Indies. . ."

He translates and publishes the orders of the Casa de Contratacion, the House of Trade in Seville, a funnel through which all trade to and from the New World must flow, so that English merchants could study its workings.

Throughout the reign of Elizabeth, but in particular in the last years of the century, the administration, from the Court to the smallest parish council, periodically sweated in the fear of "beggars coming to town" — hordes of unemployed, disease ridden and potentially violent men and women without a home or a place in society invading the frontier of respectability. When the woollen trade had a slump because of some interruption of European trade, the weavers went on the road. In the bad harvest years of 1594-97 famine forced the field labourers onto the road. Poor relief at a parish level existed but was never able to deal with a crisis and the good townsfolk resented the presence of someone else's poor and petitioned Parliament to do something about it. Hakluyt from the first, saw the colonies not only as a way of raising national pride, but as especially important in giving useful employment to our surplus people.

> Our prisons are pestered and filled with able men to serve their Country, which for small robberies are daily hanged up in great numbers, even twenty at a clap, out of one gaol! We should make it possible for them to go into the temperate and fertile parts of America, which, being within six weeks sailing of England, are yet unpossessed of any Christians, and seem to offer themselves to us, stretching nearer unto Her Majestys dominions than to any other part of Europe."

He made great efforts to persuade the Queen or any of the most interested parties like the cities of London or Bristol to sponsor regular lectures for pilots and navigators on the Spanish model. He repeatedly demonstrated the necessity for a good system of practical education in nautical matters so that longer voyages could be undertaken, with the best available knowledge of ship maintenance and of navigation.

The Principal Navigations is above all a compendium of practical hints on all aspects of coastal and island navigation which might make trading easier — the most recent maps, sketches of port installations, even details of anchorages or buoys, none of which had ever been collected together before.

Hakluyt did not get his school of navigation, but his book had an extraordinay influence. By combining the stirring adventures of the early navigators and underlining the deeds of derring-do of Queen Elizabeth's own voyagers like Hawkins, Drake and Frobisher with the commercial facts and figures of territories to be taken, mineral resources to be seized, markets to be exploited, insolent foreigners to be out-flanked, riches to be made, Hakluyt touched a raw and timely nerve. Glory and riches were waiting.

Prelude

England was ideally placed to seize them. The colonial idea took root and *The Principal Navigations* pointed to Virginia and to the West Indies ... a British commercial empire with a promise of sport in the shape of licensed piracy and a friendly Protestant God to reward good business.

2

Written With the Sword's Point

A crew of cutlass-thrusting pirates on a small ship, a sudden massacre of helpless natives, and a memorial burnt onto a fragment of wood or scraped on a standing stone, was how Jonathan Swift wrote of the idea of colonial expansion. But what was intended as satirical exaggeration in the 18th century, seems less so now that the history of European expansion and Imperial ambition has been more fully researched and related.

There may have been a time, a very short time, when the news of the first discoveries of Columbus promised the lure of precious islands in the sun, with gold as a prize, and the adventure of exploration for the love of knowledge and unknown truths about the physical world. With God as a partner in honest trade without violence, it was an ideal worthy of the High Renaissance and the energetic, curious, intrepid beings who typified Renaissance men. How quickly and sadly the ideal turned sour, becoming instead greed for easy pickings and instant wealth, the exercise of power and the exploitation of primitive peoples and places beyond the gaze of civilisation.

The West Indies is a long chain of islands sweeping like a comet's tail from the American mainland of the Florida peninsula round in a crescent to a point close to the Orinoco delta in what is now Venezuela. The chain consists of several hundred islands stretched over nearly 2,000 miles of sea and which vary in size from Cuba, which is hundreds of miles long with wide variations of climate and terrain, to isolated sea-girt rocks without shelter or natural resource. At the southern end of the chain are the islands of the Lesser Antilles forming an irregular crescent from Trinidad lying nearest to the South American mainland just above 10° Latitude North up to St. Christophers and its neighbours scattered closely together around 18° Latitude North; then the chain continues West through St. Thomas and the Virgin Islands with the last small islands within sight of Puerto Rico, the island which marks the Eastern limit of the Greater Antilles. Very few of these islands are even as big as the Isle of Wight, several are actively volcanic, and with one exception, the distance between all these islands is less than 30 miles, the one exceptional gap being between Grenada and Tobago, which was the main seaway for sailing ships to the Spanish Main. These islands to the 17th century Englishman were the Caribbee islands.

The whole chain benefitted from the North East trade winds which in the days of sail blew the ships across the Atlantic towards them and made the most easterly island group first landfall after a sea voyage of ten to twelve weeks. The wind was a hazard when, as often happened in the early navigations when measurements of latitude and longitude were frequently far from true, ships overshot the islands. Beating back against the north easterly could prolong a journey by many weeks ... a fact which many a slave trader was to regret bitterly, and used as a spur to the design of improved navigational instruments and maps and to more manoeuverable ships able to sail closer to the wind. The trade winds gave the islands a permanent windward side, the eastern, where it was mostly too dangerous to anchor, and a permanent leeward side, the western, where it was possible for ships to ride at anchor in tolerable safety. In military terms this reduced the length of coastline vulnerable to attack and made defensive measures easier to plan. The north easterlies had another strategic quality since their effect was to make it quicker to sail to the West Indies from an English port than from the mainland Spanish colonies of Mexico or Panama, a fact which was often exploited in the cat and mouse warfare of the 17th and 18th centuries.

Long before the arrival of the Europeans, the Caribbean Islands had their inhabitants, a pale brown race of Arawak Indians who spilled out from the Guianas and Venezuela on the mainland and voyaged in their long canoes throughout the islands as far as Cuba, stopping and settling where conditions were favourable. They were, it seems, a peaceful and friendly race of hunters, fishers and farmers, with a social structure not dissimilar to those tribes of the Amazon basin which have been the subject of much anthropological research and worldwide concern, in the last large primitive tribal area in the world now at risk to the exterminating embrace of modern man.

But before the Europeans reached them, the Arawaks had to face their own exterminating angels. A warlike Carib people also

7

emerged from the Orinoco basin, possibly bursting up from Brazil. They were a restless, heartless and migratory people with an unprepossessing custom of cannibalising their victims to humiliate them. With war canoes and armed to the teeth, they invaded Trinidad and massacred the unwarlike Arawaks, absorbing the younger women, moving onwards island by island, until the Arawaks who had numbered several million were reduced to thousands, stopping short of Cuba and Jamaica in the North and never landing on Barbados, perhaps because of its isolated position to the East of the main chain of islands.

These were the people who met Columbus in 1493 when he arrived in the Windwards and Leewards. They met the Spanish landing parties with force. The Spaniards were more interested in silver and gold, and after making token claims of each island with wooden markers and a ring of dead Carib riddled with crossbow arrows, they moved on towards the bigger islands where hopes of discovering minerals were better founded. Soon Mexico and Peru claimed their attention and the islands were left unsettled, or with only token garrisons, a mistake in long-term strategy which Spain was to regret in the battle for commercial empires.

The English too had visited the islands during the early years of Queen Elizabeth as they sailed through them to attack the Spaniards. West country privateers and merchants like Sir John Hawkins were among them and the accounts of these adventures, together with captured maps and ships' logs were the source of Richard Hakluyt's suggestive texts. Hakluyt's challenge, as we saw in the Prelude, was that our national destiny in some way lay in our opening up an empire in the West, giving endless opportunity for brave and ambitious Englishmen, trained in the mould of Hawkins, Drake and Cabot, using speculative capital from the merchants and gentlemen of London and providing new homes for what was then thought to be a dangerously high surplus population in England. Any expedition of the period was bound to be a costly affair, so national glory was dressed in mercantile clothing to attract the city merchants — the discovery of Eldorado whose gold mines would rival the mines of the Spaniards, a great new market for British manufacturers to the native peoples of America, a chance of finding a Western route through the Americas to tap the Asian spice trade without the long haul round by Portuguese infested Africa and India, new sources of raw materials, naval stores and other commodities for which England was dependent on European rival powers. These lures of power mixed with personal initiative, trading riches mixed with plunder, adventure with glory, were a potent brew in the social climate of the early 17th century. The Atlantic was the 17th century Europeans' Wild West, and, like the Wild West, the rash, the volatile and the lawless were the scouts, the skirmishers and the adventurers. Many disappeared, some found riches, but above all they provided information — information that many of the dreams — dreams of quick profit, of gold, of peoples eager for woollen clothing, of a hidden passage to Asia — simply did not exist, but there was a possibility of rich new lands on which plants could grow at a phenomenal rate and where an enterprising planter with suitable labour might make a rapid fortune.

Thomas Warner was one of the first Englishmen to recognise the possibilities and, more important, was able to find the resources to act. He mounted an expedition to farm a settlement on St. Christophers and from this start the movement spread to other islands.

Thomas Warner was nothing if not opportunist. As a younger son of a Suffolk gentleman of modest means, he had no expectations at home and joined the army as soon as he was old enough to do so. In the army he appears to have been successful, showing early talent for discipline and organisation, for we find him as a Captain in James I's bodyguard. As 'a good Souldier and a man of extraordinary agillety of bodie, of a good witt and one who was truly honest and freindly to all men', he was easily able to exploit his position and make useful connections at Court — the source of all advantage and favour.

In the Spring of 1620 he accompanied Captain Roger North on an expedition to the Amazon where he helped create a plantation at the mouth of the delta, in what up to that time had been considered exclusively Portuguese territory. During the late years of Queen Elizabeth's reign, Portuguese ships and Portuguese lands had been considered fair game by English privateers, but James I wished to play a different diplomatic tune. The new colony suddenly found its royal recognition withdrawn, communications with England stopped, and its leader, North, was thrown in the Tower as he visited England to plead his case.

Warner had, during this difficult time, met a Captain Paignton who had spoken highly of the fertility and climate of St. Christophers, and losing faith in the Amazon colony he decided to depart with some companions. Sailing to St. Christophers he made an agreement with a local settlement of Caribs and spent a year experimenting with tobacco which was beginning to fetch profitable prices as Europe's latest luxury. Warner then sailed back to England and coaxed a syndicate of London merchants, of whom Ralph Merrifield was the chief member, to back a more permanent plantation on the island. At the same time he recruited his Suffolk neighbour Charles Jeaffreson into the scheme.

Gathering together a group of some seventeen companions, Warner sailed to St. Christophers, landing again on January 28th, 1624, the date which marks the first permanent British settlement of the West Indies islands.

St. Christophers is one of the smallest islands in the Eastern group of Lesser Antilles. It is roughly the shape of a fish twenty two miles from head to tail and less than six miles across at its widest. In the centre, effectively cutting off East and West from direct contact, is a range of forested mountains capped by Mount Misery. Its small size was a positive advantage to the first colonists who felt able to defend it against Carib threats. Furthermore it was off the main route of Spanish fleets heading for Cartagena or Puerto Bello.

When Warner landed, he renewed contact with King Tregeman, the Carib leader with whom some sort of prior non-aggression treaty had been settled. The English began to clear land and long-sightedly to build a fort which they excused to the Caribs as a chicken house. It was not long, however, before the Caribs schemed against them. An informant brought Warner news that King Tregeman and Carib menfolk had entered one of their three to four day drinking bouts which always preceded a war party. Warner's party, heavily outnumbered, could only hope to survive by a pre-emptive attack, so according to a contemporary account:

> Like a wise man and good Souldier he tooke ye advantage of their being druncke and fell upon them by might and did kill and slay a great many of them. Amongst ye rest they slew King Tegreeman in his hammacco and runing him with their rapieres thorough ye hammacco and into the body; and others gott into their cannoes, and soe gott into other Islands amongst their neighbouring Indians and freinds".

Throughout the next hundred years the Caribs were to be pursued and killed, group by group, island by island, as they interfered, or threatened to interfere, with European settlements. Of this once proud race only a few traces remain in a reserve on Domenica and in the shape of a head or a nose, or a look, in the racial melting pot of Trinidad.

The work of planting then continued and by September the first crop of tobacco was ready to harvest. This time, however, natural disaster in the form of a hurricane struck the island, destroying the crop and the settlement. They rebuilt their log cabins and started again.

In March 1625 John Jeaffreson arrived with the ship Hopewell full of provisions and new colonists, including women and children, and Warner's wife.

The next complication for the settlers was the landing of the crew of a French privateer which needed to refit after a rough encounter with a Spanish man of war. The French skipper soon grasped the potential of the island for development and decided to settle there also. Warner needed reinforcements to counter a possible return of a Carib revenge party and at first, the need for co-operation in the face of a common foe prevented friction between French and English settlers. However, after a large force of Caribs had been successfully repulsed, a formal division of the island became necessary. The agreement provided for the English to have the centre (body of the fish) of the island, and the French the head and part of the tail. The tail fin itself consisted of salt pans and were to be considered as common property. A vital part of the deal was the provision that in the event of war between France and England, the settlements should remain neutral unless ordered directly from the sovereign governments to do otherwise. Nevertheless the division was a constant source of friction and St. Christophers remained until 1783 the flashpoint for Anglo-French rivalry.

The settlement of the French and rumours of a further threat to his fortunes from a rival combine of merchants and courtiers hastened Thomas Warner's departure to England to try and get official — which meant royal — authority for his fledgling colony. It was a daunting mission, for the throne was no longer occupied by James I, with whom he had some personal contact, but by his son Charles I who had surrounded himself with a new and venal group of courtiers led by George Villiers, Earl of Buckingham, who effectively blocked all approaches to the King for favours or offices which did not pass through him, and who mismanaged everything he touched. "What is in it for me and mine?" was the first question for any petitioner. The group of titled courtiers around the throne sold their patronage and favour with the King to the highest and noblest bidder, and the King in turn accepted the best offer made to him. The kind of grant Warner aspired to was a proprietary letters patent which would confer hereditary rights to him on his colony in return for defined liabilities to the home government, either an annual rental or a share of product shipped to London, or both. But Warner was not even a Knight, and patents seemed open only to Earls. So he obtained the best he could, which was a commission as Royal Lieutenant of the group of four islands of St. Christophers, Nevis, Montserrat and Barbados,

11

in effect a Governorship, and royal protection for the trading syndicate led by Merrifield, on terms revokable at the King's pleasure. The royal pleasure was a slippery concept to grasp and even more slippery to hold on to. Warner knew it well, and was dextrous enough for the task. As a member of the King's body-guard he would have learnt as much about the mechanism of royal patronage as anyone outside the charmed circle of intimate courtiers, and so while showing gratitude for the favour he had received, he took active steps elsewhere to reinforce and improve his prospects. First he appears to have solicited the help of the Lord Treasurer, John Ley, Earl of Marlborough, a man sufficiently venal and powerful to be able to obtain a proprietary grant.

The Earl of Marlborough was another sharp operator. Rather than buy a grant, he obtained an option on it and then sold his option to a third party, the Earl of Carlisle — apparently with Warner's consent.

The Earl of Carlisle was a Scottish courtier who came to London in the wake of James I. At Court he was a bluff, jovial character who was famous for his expensive tastes and lavish style of living, whether on Court business or his own. Unfortunately he always spent more than he could obtain and was always heavily in debt. For a fee he too could be bought to do favours at Court — the bigger the favour the bigger the fee; the bigger the fee, the less his scruples. At this particular time some of his biggest creditors were prominent London merchants who were themselves interested in investing in new and promising island colonies. For themselves therefore, and also as a protection against a possibility of default by the good Earl of Carlisle, they proposed a scheme in which he would become the front-man for a new syndicate to own and exploit a whole group of islands, including St. Christophers. All parties recognised that if such a bid succeeded the possibilities for lucrative trade and extortion were enormous. Where did this leave Thomas Warner? We have to infer from later events that he was a party to the proposed patent, or at least promised his co-operation should it be given, and that part of his price was a Knighthood and confirmation of his holdings on St. Christophers. As for his own merchant backers, led by Ralph Merrifield, they too must have felt secure because when Warner returned to the West Indies in April 1626, the syndicate had been strengthened by the recruitment of Maurice Thompson, head of a London export house, who later became one of the most import-ant West Indian merchants.

So Warner sailed away while negotiations between Carlisle and the King proceeded. (Charles was "an immoderate lover of the

Scottish" and Carlisle was a Scot). He took with him three new ships, a hundred new recruits, and the aura of confidence which the hope of great expectations gave him. Already the Warner family was moving up the social ladder and acquiring a fortune in a very satisfactory way.

In July 1627 the Earl of Carlisle persuaded Charles I to sign the papers he required — Letters Patent, making him absolute lord proprietor of the Caribee Islands listed, to be known as Carlisle Province. The Crown received an annual rental and a percentage of all gold or silver found. In return, the Earl was empowered to make laws, elect judges with wide powers of life and death over the settlers and their servants. He had various lucrative appointments and posts to offer to those he wished to oblige, and honours to bestow. Above all, there were trading privileges for his merchant friends. It was, in short, tantamount to a license to print money, in favour of the London backers rather than the planters, a point which the planters were not slow to appreciate and resist.

The formal structure of colonial rule was to evolve slowly out of many experiments and experiences in different climates and situations. The arguments are well presented elsewhere. The Proprietary Patent was primarily an instrument for making money. Charles I, always short of finance, was both unwise and unscrupulous in his methods of raising it. He saw no constitutional problem in using the royal prerogative when offering pieces of the world map, which no-one else had specifically claimed, to suitable bidders and giving them immense hereditary powers over people and places nominally still his subjects; it was after all, money for nothing; he was giving nothing away and might even gain an asset which he could pull back at a later stage. And because of the vagueness of maps and the confused spelling of distant places he might even be able to sell a place twice, or create a commercial confusion which he could later exploit.

Flushed with success at his London coup and armed with his new authority, Thomas Warner began to organise St. Kitts to his own way. First he set about selling leases which would effectively attach fledgling planters to the land and raise useful revenue. Planters were reluctant and untrusting, but the carrot of tax-free trade with the mother country was finally persuasive. Warner then turned the island into an armed camp. Certainly there was a real threat of imminent attack from the Caribs, from the French with whom the island was shared, but above all from the Spaniards; a careful Governor had to take suitable precautions, build forts, maintain defences and train a militia. Warner neglected none of these duties. Sir Henry Colt, a visiting trader and raider wrote . . .

> St. Christophers . . . live like unto soldyers, ther court of garde appoynted them, ther centinells orderly placed. Noe man ther cann stir, or wander a nights; yett are ther harbours moor secured by shippinge then yours. Ther governour knowes yt a soldyer must as well keep gards when an enemy is farr of, as when he is neer at hand".

But Warner used the excuse of military preparedness to impose a regime of personal tyranny, the better to exploit the planters. The Governor made the official appointments, chose the judges, to a large extent made the laws. There were no representative institutions through which planters could voice grievances, there was no appeal to a higher court in the case of injustice. Punishment was summary and often cruel.

No-one had ever pretended that pioneering in the new colonies was likely to be a bed of roses. The rewards were uncertain, life precarious and cheap. But at home, for many people, things were little better and there was not even an outside chance of gaining a fortune. So recruits were never lacking for early colonial ventures, and they were a very varied company indeed. There were young men of good family and little prospects, second and third sons hopeless of inheritance, there were criminals putting themselves beyond the reach of the law, and men whose style of life had accumulated a mill-stone of debt from which they hoped to escape. There were religious dissenters seeking freedom from an intolerant establishment, or a society not prepared to admit them on equal terms — Catholics, once hopeful of privileges under the Stuarts but outlawed in the aftermath of the Gunpowder Plot and other attacks on the King and his ministers; Puritans of many shades, frustrated at their failure to obtain fundamental reforms in the established church, seeking a place to worship according to their individual conscience or to be free to organise their own church. Then there were the common people, the poor, the disinherited, the out of work. For them life was in a very true sense "nasty, brutish and short". Wages were low, the economy in the reign of the first two Stuarts was in almost continual crisis. There were bad depressions where three quarters of a million, or 20% of the population, lived at starvation level, without the life-line of effective charity or any form of national assistance. Disease also added its formidable toll of suffering. The threat of bubonic plague was never far away and a number of alarming outbreaks in the early years of the century added a fearful dimension to city life. Somehow the more prosperous classes felt that the armies of

14

beggars, out of work and wandering poor were to blame for the spread of killer disease *and* the economic ills of the country. In the absence of work at home, any measures to persuade or force them into industrious work overseas and remove them both from the poor rate and from sight were welcome. As the essayist Bacon wrote, it would be "a double commodity, in the avoidance of people here, and in making use of them there".

The untamed islands needed labour, a great deal of labour, to make them habitable and profitable. Attempts to train local Indians, either Arawak or Carib, were disastrous. The Spanish on the mainland had made the experiment and failed. The English were no more successful. Excessive labour, poor diet and above all, imported European diseases killed the Arawaks or Caribs rapidly. There was as yet no tradition of negro slavery, so the obvious source of workers was in the pool of rootless poor whites back home. The employing planters or their promoters went about recruiting labour in different ways. The indentured servant was a man or woman who, in return for their passage, signed a legal contract, binding them by law to work overseas for a minimum period, usually three to five years, at the end of which they would have a small grant of land to develop on their own account. Redemptioners made a deal with the captain of the ship to pay back their passage on arrival in the colony or be liable to be sold to the highest bidder.

If the lot of the early planter, faced with unknown soil and fickle leadership was a tough one, life for the white servant was barbarous and little short of slavery. The smaller islands like St. Christophers were glorified floating prisons from which escape was virtually impossible. Instead of enclosing walls there were uncharted waters and any ships which called were in the hands of the owners, or the government, and therefore usually hostile. The white servant was utterly at the mercy of the planters to be worked like a pack horse, or like a slave. An eye-witness account of early Barbados relates:

> If they complain they are beaten by an Overseer; if they resist their time is doubled. I have seen an Overseer beat a Servant with a cane about the head till the blood has followed for an offence that is not worth the speaking of"

Even the promise of land was more often a trick. The best lands in the smaller islands were reserved for the owners and their nominees; the less attractive land by the lesser planters without influence; servants of fair-minded owners might get an uneconomic or boggy patch or two, but most owners found ready excuse for defaulting on their obligations altogether.

Not surprisingly, when it came to squaring up to an outside enemy, the servants as a whole were reluctant partners. Sir Henry Colt whose pithy narrative of a voyage to Barbados and St. Christophers in 1631 illuminates the situation tartly.

> Certainly I am persuaded St. Christophers to be an enterprise of great difficulty to attempt. If ye men servants who are ye greatest numbers could be brought to fight ... But these servants of ye planters rather desyer ye Spaniards might come, yt by itt they might be freed, then any willingnesse they shew to defend their masters. Ther was two of these men yt ridd uppon a wooden horse with weights of ther feet by ye command of ye Governour for words to ye like effect . . ."

Nevertheless recruitment went rapidly ahead. By the start of 1629, 3000 people had been shipped to the island. Warner was also well satisfied with his financial progress. As early as December 1627 he was sending home 20,000 lbs. of tobacco and a month later Ralph Merrifield was reporting the arrival of 10,000 lbs. weight. The only cloud on that horizon was that the development of new tobacco growing colonies would swamp the European market and depress the growers' price. Thoughts of protective regulations began to be heard.

In the following year, the Earl of Carlisle obtained a second Patent which in the main confirmed the first and helped him overthrow a rival syndicate which had believed itself the rightful owners of Barbados — a conspiratorial manoeuvre in which Warner certainly had a part and reaped rich reward but which we can only mention in passing. The major change in the new Patent was in relation to the period of custom and tax-free trading promised the planters in the earlier Patent. In a clause full of bland deceit, it gives the Earl of Carlisle the right to all those taxes which would otherwise have become due to the Crown on all goods to and from the islands in his province, and to take and use them for his own ends. The merchant syndicate behind the Earl was greatly strengthened at the expense of the planters who, it will be remembered, had only recently bought leases on their plantations because of the tax-free incentive. In the most cynical way, Thomas Warner and his staff began to collect the new revenue. For Warner personally there was a Knighthood and a new appointment as Governor of St. Kitts for life.

In 1629, while Warner was in London, the colony was almost destroyed by an unexpected and large scale Spanish raid. The regular convoy on its way to the Spanish Main had been instructed to make a show of force against any intruder settlements they found in the Leewards and re-establish Spanish control there.

St. Christophers was well defended but the indentured servants refused to fight and swam out to the Spanish ships with details of all the defences, and the planters were forced to surrender, crowded aboard the fleet and sent back to England. The plantations were laid waste and hostages taken back to Spain where they remained in prison for five years as no-one would pay their ransom.

St. Christophers was not completely lost. Some planters had fled to the woods and waited for the Spanish ships to leave. Others returned as soon as released by the Spaniards in distant ports. Warner lost no time in bringing out reinforcements from England and re-established his authority with even greater thoroughness than before. Small planters suffered most, having no reserves to fall back on in such difficult times, and the richer planters took over their holdings. This was a pattern to be repeated all over the Indies, the big got bigger, the weak were squeezed out. Taxes were onerous and often arbitrarily increased. Food was frequently scarce when ships failed to arrive in time. Rebellion was never far below the surface. On one occasion a man was hanged simply for defaming Colonel Jeaffreson and Warner had to call on the French to help him suppress the rising which followed. Some of the trouble was indeed the fault of the planters. Imbued with the frontier spirit and courageous even to foolhardiness they were at the same time a quarrelsome lot, giving way reluctantly to any form of discipline or regulation. Heavy drinking made matters worse as Sir Henry Colt writes during his visit . . .

> You are all younge men, & of good desert, if you would but bridge ye excesse of drinkinge, together with ye quarelsome condition of your fyery spiritts. You are devourers upp of hott waters & such good distillers thereof . . . But ye worst of all was your mainfold quarrels. Your younge and hott bloods should nott have oyle added to increase ye flame, but rather cold water to quench it."

As wealth accumulated Warner began to look beyond St. Kitts. St. Kitts could support no more colonists, and the syndicate's fief included many other so far untenanted islands, many of which were suitable for colonisation. Warner too had a growing family of sons, one of whom was half Carib, and a man with his wealth and ambitions could not fail to think in dynastic terms — plantation and appointments for the boys as they came of age.

Nevis, the nearest island to St. Kitts, was colonised sometime in 1628 by a group of about one hundred mainly St. Kitts planters and servants backed by a new syndicate in London, although still within the interest of the Earl of Carlisle. The leader was Anthony Hilton from Durham and he became the first Governor.

Antigua and Montserrat were both colonised in the mid 1630's. Warner had been "pestered with many controversies of the planters", an important element of which were religious. Toleration between different religious persuasions was no easier to obtain in a colonial setting than in England and so Warner determined to get rid of the most rabid of the extremists by shipping them to other islands. Montserrat was settled by a party of Irish Roman Catholics, Antigua by a party of Puritans. Fortified no doubt by their respective Gods, they both flourished and prospered.

Two other colonising expeditions arising from Warner's grand strategy, were less successful. An attempt to settle St. Lucia, an island not far from Barbados, provoked such bitter retaliation from the Caribs that the colonists were almost exterminated. A similar expedition to Marigalante led by Sir Thomas Warner himself, survived until 1653, but was also over-whelmed by the Caribs. Not all Sir Thomas touched turned to gold and controversy pursued him to the end of his life. Barbados refused, at all times, to recognise his authority in anything and the legal wrangles about its ownership continued well after his death and the scattering of the Carlisle syndicate.

The Warner family became a rich and influential one in several islands, and even migrated to Virginia where Augustus Warner founded another rich branch of the family. Philip was founder of the Antiguan branch where he had extensive sugar estates. He was a reforming Governor and left a strong team of sons, all of whom became involved in West Indian politics and commerce. Ashton Warner of Antigua sent his elder son to England to be educated, and he became a distinguished 18th century surgeon operating at Guys Hospital and becoming the first member of the Royal College of Surgeons. This year there is still a Warner on the senior medical staff at Guys.

In the 19th century Warner continues the family tradition as President of the Council in Antigua, while Aucher Warner, as Attorney General of Trinidad was an elegant advocate of Asian immigration. Those of the family not actually planting found high legal or administrative office in the West Indies. Today Warners still farm in the Leewards and while no single branch of the family is ostentatiously rich, the energetic and acquisitive founder made certain, one might almost say planned, that his multiplying family would, natural disaster permitting, enjoy an affluent fortune.

But in the 20th century, the best known offshoot of the Warner tree was Pelham Warner, famous cricketer. Captain for England in 1903-4 against Australia in a series where England brought home the ashes, and who died in 1963 . . .

3

The Master Planters

James Drax, a young Englishman with a few hundred pounds, sailed from the Port of London for Barbados in the late 1620's and there made a family fortune. He was from the start a born survivor. The story is told in the old histories of how he and his party of seven or eight companions had to shelter for some time in caves on the island and eke out their small provisions by hunting. There were wild hogs left by the Portuese years previously as a living larder, and iguana lizards, but few birds. The party set about clearing a piece of land in which they planted tobacco. The crop flourished, Drax found a ship to take him back to London with it and sold it profitably. He then returned to Barbados with more provisions and fifty men which enabled him to start building up a substantial estate. He lost no time. Within ten years or so he was a wealthy man and about to make the step which turned him into a veritable merchant prince.

The British had settled Barbados a few years before Drax arrived. It was uninhabited except by its riotous rout of animal and insect life, just another island that the Spaniards, who regarded the Caribbean as their preserve, had neglected to occupy. But the fight over rights of ownership between contending groups of courtiers and merchants bedevilled the effective settlement of the island for many years. Conflicting parties hijacked it from each other on numerous occasions. Warner of St. Kitts was himself a party to these disputes, whose motive was greed and whose settlement would resolve in simple terms who would have the richest reward. That is what colonies of the period were about. In Barbados these tensions were fuelled by the struggle in England between the King and Parliament. Political refugees from both sides fled to the Indies and formed into passionate cliques, quite

20

prepared to oust each other in the name of the King or Pariament, Cavalier or Roundhead as the parties called themselves, with the alluring promise to whichever party won, of benefitting by the total expropriation of the losers' goods and estates.

But planting and building had to go on regardless. Barbados was a small island, about the size of the Isle of Wight, with a wide variety of climate and soil, upland and lowland, marsh and crag, windswept rocky coastline and balmy bay. To actually find it, with the navigational knowledge of the time was difficult enough, because it was not part of the Leeward chain but isolated from it to the East. Early 17th century sea captains wrote of how easy it was to miss altogether, and because of the prevailing winds, never get back. "Finding it", one of them wrote, "is like throwing a sixpence down somewhere on Newmarket Heath, then telling a rider on horseback that it is 13 miles due West of him now and ordering him to go and find it." It was some fifteen weeks sailing time from London, from the source of provisions, equipment and labour.

There was not time to sit back and be complacent. Before anything at all could be planted, the ground had to be cleared. At first Barbados was heavily forested — a mass of trees. With only hand tools of indifferent quality, a great deal of back-breaking labour was needed. As with St. Kitts recruits were found in England, naively selling themselves for a pittance for a fixed term of years, in the hope of eventually becoming wealthy proprietors themselves. The lists of these men collected on various official records show them to be heart-rendingly young. Out of a list of a hundred leaving London in 1638, thirty are under fifteen, several under twelve, and almost all the rest under twenty five. Other lists give the same kind of results. But recruitment of free white servants was not quick enough. A market in prisoners was organised, for planters did not care greatly where their labour came from. A planter could write encouragingly, "no gaolbird can be so incorrigible, but there is hope of his conformity here, as well as his preferment, which some have happily experimented". Prisoners from England, due to be hanged, or sentenced to long terms of imprisonment were sold as a job lot to a Courtier or other Government official as a speculation, and sold off the ship direct to planters in the West Indies. To "Barbadoes someone" became a household word. Still there was not enough labour, so the men whose money was invested in the success of the colonies turned to black slaves — the "black ebony" of Africa.

Sugar and slavery both entered the British West Indies at Barbados, and the wealth which they generated provoked an almost instantaneous revolution in the organisation and prosperity of the island. The credit for this is usually attributed to James Drax and to the Dutch.

In the first half of the 17th century, the Dutch had become the carriers and the bankers of much of Europe. Amsterdam was a highly developed import-export market and an important centre of credit and capital. For a long time they had traded with the Portuguese colonies along the North East coast of what is now Brazil, carrying their sugar to Europe and selling it for them, providing equipment and expertise and, above all, slaves for the plantations. They had even planted settlements on their own account and they traded with the newly-settled West Indian islands in many ways. The Dutch and British in the Caribbean were good friends. The events in outline were as follows: at the start of the forties, the Portuguese decided to reassert their territorial rights in Brazil and expel the Dutch. Dutch refugees came to Barbados and offered expertise in setting up sugar plantations. The Dutch were helpful in other ways. England was locked in the grip of Civil War and supplies from home, never bountiful at the best of these early times, came to a virtual halt. The Dutch provided the expertise of sugar cultivation, offered capital for buying machinery, sold the colonists African slaves to make the sugar, bought the grown sugar and carried it to Europe, where they made a good profit.

Drax was already a successful planter. To become that he had learnt a number of important lessons. Lesson number one was how to survive. No health manual, no School of Tropical Medicine, virtually no knowledge except hearsay, culled from the footnotes of captains' diaries, was available for the Tropical traveller. No prophylactic, no anti-septic, no antedote existed against tropical disease or bite, and, worse, the very nature of disease was unsuspected — how to cope with extreme heat and humidity where a knife rusted in the sheath within ten minutes of sharpening, or the dry prickly heat of a scorching mid-day; how to eat and relax and sleep in an environment of teeming insect life, of scavenger ants, giant cockroaches, mosquitoes and jiggers; how to preserve food in an iceless and refrigerator-less age when commodities had to be shipped all the way from England; how to cope with the psychological problems of alienation, loneliness and living on perpetual guard from one's companions and servants.

Lesson number two was how to farm in the unfamiliar natural conditions — a year without familiar seasons; a soil prodigal in its fertility and in its natural pests; an environment where animal husbandry needs a whole new set of rules; what to grow which

22

could be sent on a long sea journey in good condition *and* fetch a good price.

Lesson number three was how to manage the business and economic management of his venture. In theory, the Government, the island proprietors, the merchants with whom he traded wanted him to succeed — wanted all pioneer colonists to succeed — but, in practice, there were many contradictory and changing pressures which had to be met as they occurred. Was it always wise to try and sell one's goods in London when perhaps a Dutch merchant consistently offered a better price? Must he always arrange his credit needs in the home country when perhaps he could get better terms elsewhere? Could he invariably trust his correspondents to deal honestly with him? What morality or business ethic was currently applicable — if not dog eat dog!

Lesson number four — politics. The planters were plain and passionate men with their share, perhaps more than their share, of the political and religious prejudices of the time — most of them had left England because of their strongly held principles. Now they found themselves in a virtually privately owned fief of an absentee courtier whose nominated officer made his own laws and appointed his own lieutenants. Worse than that, because of a frivolous lack of responsibility, the King had fixed his seal on two different and opposed proprietory patents covering Barbados, so that two courtier led syndicates believed themselves to be the true owners. Since the openly confessed objective of most planters was to make their fortunes and move on, since the commercial success of the venture must override all others, a flexible, pragmatic kind of politics was commonsense, and this is what Drax adopted. Other planters who let their passions rule fared less well.

Lesson five — how to get the best work out of an unwilling labour force. The answer the planters arrived at was naked coercion, and brutal punishment for disobedience — the English planters developed the system enthusiastically. At first the victims were the poor whites, the English, Scots and Irish who had volunteered as indentured servants, then, as recruiting became harder, shiploads of transported convicts. The work gang supervised by the whip-carrying overseer, the degraded living conditions, the brutal punishment for infringement of discipline were developed before black slaves were introduced. Such a system would not have been possible in the home country, but Barbados was an artificial community with only two classes, masters and servants. It was a long way from home, and the line of communication was a fragile one. Who was there to protest? And since the Court and the country's commercial leadership were interested parties, who was there to listen? In isolation, and with an easy conscience therefore, the West Indian colonists perfected the forced labour camp system in all its sadistic glory and when at last the time came to buy slaves, they adapted the system quite naturally to the more extreme conditions of slavery.

Finally, lesson six — to cope with lady luck. Brian Edwards, an 18th century planter and historian of the Indies summed it up.

> A West Indian property is a species of lottery. As such, it gives birth to a spirit of adventure and enterprise, and awakens extravagent hopes and expectations; — too frequently terminating in perplexity and disappointment.

To pioneer planters like Drax, the transition from servants to slaves was a simple step. In cold terms of profit and loss, a slave once bought was owned for a life-time, an indentured servant was owned for a term of years only, after which he was to be given freedom and a smallholding. There were no ethical problems, no religious scruples, certainly no sentiment. As far as crops were concerned, Drax was also open to ideas of change. Tobacco, cotton and indigo were indeed in big demand in Europe, but the Barbados tobacco crop was consistently proving difficult. Top quality harvests eluded the planters and the English complained of Barbadan tobacco's earthy flavour. The most enterprising planters were in fact ready for a change at the very moment when it became realistically possible.

So while England entered a Civil War to end the 'Eleven Years Tyranny' of arbitrary royal Government, the Dons of Barbados as they were in future to be known, led their own social revolution to establish a much more oppressive and alien system, the society of master and slave.

Records of the first sugar years are very rare and we have to rely on Richard Ligon, a refugee from England who, "having lost (by a Barbarous Riot)" all that he had, decided he had "to famish or fly" and took the first ship that he could to another part of the world. Chance brought him to Barbados in 1647 where he settled for some years as a planter under the protection of one of the biggest, Thomas Modyford. Returning to England in the early 1650's he wrote a short account of the early history and current economic state of Barbados which is invaluable to an understanding of the first gold rush years of sugar.

When Ligon landed in 1647 he saw "that the great work of Sugar-making was but newly practised by the inhabitants there", but "by the time I left the island, which was in 1650, they were much better'd". In fact he writes:

> Sugar-making . . . is now grown the soul of Trade in this Island.
> Several of the more enterprising planters were already very rich. Colonell James Drax, whose beginning upon that island, was founded upon stock not exceeding 300/Sterling, has raised his fortune to such a height, as I have heard him say, that he would not look towards England, with a purpose to remain there, the rest of his life, till he were able to purchase an estate, of tenne thousand pound land yearly; which he hop'd in a few years to accomplish, with what he was then owner of; and all this by the plant of sugar. Colonell Thomas Modyford, has often told me, that he had taken a Resolution to himselfe, not to set his face for England, till he made his voyage and employment there worth him a hundred thousand pounds Sterling, and all by this Sugar plant. And these, were men of piercing sights and profound judgments, as any I have known in that way of management.

It also makes the point quite clearly that the planters regarded their life in the tropics as a temporary sojourn. Ligon put the white population at about 50,000 and describes the social structure and conditions.

> The island is divided into three sorts of men, viz Masters, Servants and slaves. The slaves and their posterity, being subject to their Masters for ever, are kept and preserv'd with greater care than the servants, who are theirs but for five years, according to the law of the island. So that for the time, the servants have the worser lives, for they are put to very hard labour, ill lodging, and their dyet very slight.
> Truly, I have seen such cruelty done there to Servants, as I did not think one Christian could have done to another.

On the whole, Ligon is an admirer of the successful planters, so his evidence must be seen as objective. A French priest, Father Biet, who visited the island in 1654 only a year or so later confirms the cruel dilemma of the servant. "All are very badly treated" he writes.

Ligon describes the purchase of slaves . . .

> When they are brought to us, the Planters buy them out of the Ship, where they find them stark naked, and therefore cannot be deceived in any outward deformity. They choose them as they do Horses in a Market; the stronger, youthfullest, and most beautiful yield the greatest prices. Thirty pounds Sterling is the price for the best man Negro; and twenty-five, twenty-six or twenty-seven pounds for a Woman; the children are at easier rates . . . the most of them are neer Beasts as may be, setting their souls aside . . ."

25

And their diet:

> Potatoes, Bonavist, Loblolly, as also of the bone meat, viz, Porke, salt Fish and powder'd beefe, which came thither by sea, from forraine parts, in so much as the Negroes were allowed each man two Maquerels a weeke and every woman one, which were given out to them on Saturday in the evening, after they had their allowance of Plantines, which was everyone a large bunch, or two little ones, to serve them for a weeks provision; and if any cattle dyed by mischance, or by any disease, the servants eat the bodies, and the Negroes the skines, head and intrails which was divided amongst them by the overseers; or any horse, then the whole bodies of them were distributed amongst the Negroes, and that they thought a high feast, with which, poor soules they were contented; and the drinke to the servants with this dyet, nothing but Mobbie, and sometimes a little Beveridge, but the Negroes nothing but faire water . . .

Father Biet is more caustic:

> as for their food, there is no nation which feeds its slaves as badly as the English because for all meals the slaves only get potatoes which serve them as their bread, their meat, their fish, in fact, everything . . . they are only given meat one time in the year, namely Christmas Day, which is the only holiday observed in this island.

In contrast Colonel Drax, says Ligon, lives like a prince and describes in detail a dinner party at the Drax Household which I cannot resist quoting in full as an illustration of sheer opulence and contrast with the last two quotes.

> First then (because beefe being the greatest rarity in the Island, especially such as this is) I will begin with it, and of that sort there are these dishes at either messe, a Rumpe boyl'd, a Chine roasted, a large piece of the brest roasted, the Cheeks bak'd, of which is a dish to either messe, the tongue and part of the tripes minc'd for Pyes, season'd with sweet Herbs finely minc'd, suet, Spice, and currans; the legges, pallets and other ingredients for an Olio Podrido to either messe, a dish of Marrow-bones, so here are 14 dishes at the Table and all of beefe; and this he intends as the great Regalio, to which he invites his fellow planters; who having well eaten of it, the dishes are taken away, and another Course brought in, which is a Potato pudding, a dish of Scots collips of a legge of Porke, as good as any in the world, a fricasy of the same, a dish of boyl'd Chickens, a shoulder of younge Goate drest with his blood and tyme, a Kid with a pudding in his belly, a sucking Pig, which is there the fattest whitest and sweetest in the world, with the fragrant sauce of the brains, salt, sage and Nutmeg done with Claret wine, a shoulder of Mutton which is there a rare dish, a Pasty of the side of a young Goate, and a side of a fat young Shot upon it, well season'd with Pepper and salt, and with some Nutmeg,

a loyne of Veale, to which there wants no sauce being so well finisht
with Oranges, Lymons, and Lymes, three young Turkies in a dish, two
Capons, of which sort I have seen some extreme large and very fat, two
henns with eggs in a dish, four Ducklings, eight Turtle Doves and three
Rabbets; and for cold bak'd meats, two Muscovie Ducks larded, and
season'd well with pepper and salt; and these being taken off the Table,
another course is set on, and that is of Westphalia or Spanish bacon, dried
Neats Tongues, Botargo, pickled Oysters, Caviare, Anchovies, Olives and
(intermixt with these) Custards, Creams, some alone, some with preserves
of Plantines, Banana, Guavers, put in, and those preserv'd alone by them-
selves, Cheese-cakes, Puffes, which are to be made with English flower, and
bread, for the Cassavie will not serve for this kind of Cookerie; sometimes
Tansies, sometimes Froizes, or Amulets, and for fruite, Plantines,
Bananoes, Guavers, Milions, prickled Peare, Anchove Peare, Prickled
Apple, Custard Apple, water Milions, and Pines worth all that went before.
To this meat you seldome faile of this drink, Mobbie, Beveridge, Brandy,
Kill-Divell, Drink of the Plantine, Claret wine, White wine, and Renish
wine, Sherry, Canary, Red sack, wine of Fiall, with all Spirits that come
from England . . .

By 1654, when Father Biet wrote, Drax had over 200 slaves
working his sugar plantation and his style was that of a grandee.
Father Biet describes his departure on a visit to England.

he was accompanied to the place where the ship was to embark by more
than two hundred of the island's most important people, well mounted
and marching two by two in a column headed by the Governor and
Colonel Drax. As he arrived at the embarkation place, the ship fired a
volley of all its cannons, and, having been put in the launch to go out to
the vessel, all the persons accompanying him fixed their pistols. . .

A few years earlier Ligon sets out a long list of imported commodities mostly of a utilitarian kind, together with a number of
modest luxuries. Father Biet's observations tell of an advance
of affluence amongst the rich planters which is quite remarkable.

They come here in order to become wealthy. The ladies and young
women are as well dressed as in Europe, and they economise on nothing
to dress well. One will not find it difficult to pay eight or ten pounds of
sugar in order to buy a bit of silk lace. One can judge by this little thing
what they will do in order to have a suit of clothes. For the cut of one very
simple dress coat a tailor is paid one hundred pounds of sugar. One
furnishes his house sumptuously. Things that are the finest in England and
elsewhere are found in the Island. Men and women go well-mounted on
very handsome horses which are covered with very rich saddle-cloths. The
extravagence of the table is not less. Everything is there in abundance. . .

Large planters assumed a kind of baronial independence, they assumed the role of a master class. Such law as existed, even when at last the Crown assumed the Government of the Island, while nominally the Law of England, was bent to the interests of the masters. Although Sunday was punctiliously observed by the white population, Christianity went no further. Lipservice may have been paid to official morality, but it was but a thin mask covering the almost complete breakdown of private morality. Because there were so few white women on the island, adultery, incest and homosexuality were common, and the sexual exploitation of female slaves became common. White folk lived, as one visitor said, perhaps ironically, "at the height of pleasure".

Nevertheless wrote Ligon, the masters "are men of great abilities and parts, otherwise they could not go through, with such great works as they undertake; the managing of one of their Plantations, being a work of such latitude as will require a very good head-piece, to put in order, and continue it so."

"Sugar planting", wrote Bryan Edwards over a century and a half later, "is a sort of adventure in which the man that engages, must engage deeply. There is no medium, and very seldom the possibility of retreat." What was true of Jamaica in the years of prosperity was especially true at the point of departure.

The sugar plantation was, in effect, a factory in the fields. The centre of it was the Cane Crusher and the Boiling plant with all the subsidiary tackle-filling room, Still-house and Curing-house. These were substantial capital items with many and various moving parts having to be kept in good repair and needing their spares available at short notice. To justify the cost of such machinery needed a substantial acreage of sugar, ripening field by field in steady succession. Sugar cane grew best in well-prepared and weeded fields. Once at its peak of ripeness, it had to be cut and crushed within hours or it lost all its valuable juices. Planting, weeding and cutting were precisely timed operations, employing a great deal of labour. One can see immediately why such an operation could only be undertaken by men with capital to risk, or the record of previous success as an entrepreneur which would permit a merchant or a syndicate to offer credit.

On Barbados a few hundred planters quickly attempted to dominate the new industry. They elbowed out the small planter, virtually commandeering the best land. They thought so highly of the value of land under sugar that they eliminated all other crops, even preferring to buy in food stuffs for themselves and their workers, than waste precious money-making fields on such things. In this they were encouraged by English merchants who saw a new and growing market for English goods. When indentured servants came to their full term and demanded land, there was now no land to give them, the alternatives were starvation or migration to other islands or to colonies on the main land. Over 20,000 men and women left Barbados before the end of the century. More brutally, planters might attempt to work servants to death before they could be freed, or alternatively find excuses for punishment which took the form of doubling their term of servitude.

As more slaves took over from white servants the balance between free white and exploited black shifted, until there were many more blacks than white. Rebellion was never far below the surface and the white minority became increasingly uneasy. The Militia on the island kept in readiness for possible attack. The sea now seemed the main and only safety barrier against possible revolt. In such a situation they fell back on men like Christopher Codrington, nephew of James Drax, a fire-eating young planter-warrior who wanted nothing better to do than sharpen up the island's defences, both outward-facing, or from insurrection from within.

The Codringtons were an old West Country family of squires. In Gloucestershire they were esteemed as "men of good note" in the reign of Edward II. In 1415 John Codrington fought at Agincourt with Henry V and became his standard bearer. The first Christopher Codrington, whom we have to call Christopher I, came to Barbados in 1628, built up an estate from small beginnings and married James Drax's sister, Frances. Christopher II was born in 1640 and brought up on his father's estate in a setting of opulence and naked aggression. The wealthiest planters like the Drax's, the Codringtons, Modyfords, Alleynes, even political opponents like Edward and Humphrey Walrond met at carousing feasts where food and drink were consumed in vast quantities and special slave girls were reserved for the principal guests. There were after all certain matters on which they could all agree.

Before Christopher II was 26, and already a militant competitive planter, he was chosen to be a member of the island's ruling council. At 29 he was made deputy-Governor, being "of debonnaire liberal humour". He undertook and carried out with flair a major re-organisation of the island's fortification and bullied his colleagues for assistance, but he was dismissed for quarreling with the King's new representative three years later. Immediately he was elected to the Assembly by the planters whose official platform it was, he continued an abrasive and critical campaign, against a new wave of arbitrary Government decrees originating in London, and when he had had enough, decided to transfer any fresh planting activities to the Leeward Islands. In his private capacity, together with his brother, he put in hand plantations in Antigua and on the island of Barbuda. The successful transfer of sugar planting techniques to Antigua and their adoption by planters there is credited to Codrington.

In 1688 when James II fled from England and the Glorious and bloodless Revolution of William and Mary saved the country for the Protestants, Codrington found himself acting Governor of all the scattered Leeward Islands, and then officially Captain-General. His own personal treasury enabled him to act effectively and quickly against Jacobite elements in Montserrat and Antigua and to hit and neutralise the French in their vulnerable islands before they were able to co-ordinate any kind of offensive against the British. In so doing, General Codrington showed powers of strategic command of a high order. But despite all the excellent projects he set on foot and his notable military successes, there was throughout the later years of his life a considerable ground-swell of protest and bitterness at his personal despotism; certain powerful planters had their feathers unforgivably ruffled and a clever intrigue was mounted against him in which he was accused of high treason. He died with the accusations still unresolved. He was, however, one of the richest planters and his son's inheritance was enormous.

Christopher III was a most attractive and complex man, one of the few West Indians who has received biographical treatment. Educated in England, he was a brilliant academic success at Oxford, but as a very rich son and heir, lived a full and vivid social life, even sponsoring an expensive attempt to revive from the Age of Chivalry the art of riding The Great Horse amongst the young gentlemen of the University. He was elected on merit to a Fellow-ship of All Souls and began a lifelong interest in the collecting of rare old books, for which his own private income was more than sufficient. But he had a liberal dash of his father's military tastes and he was ambitious to go to war. He joined King William's Flanders campaign as a junior officer where promotion soon brought him to the King's notice. When General Codrington died, King William remembered the dashing Colonel and appointed him to the daunting post of Governor-General of the Leewards. He agreed with a great deal of reluctance but, moved finally, one would like to think, by the desire to clear his father's name and reputation, he instituted a rule of uncompromising honesty and enlightenment — perhaps also for the sheer awkward challenge of it. Bryan Edwards, the planter historian, says simply that he was "a gentleman distinguished for his attainments in polite literature" and passes on to the next subject. Even the Dictionary of National Biography gives more lineage to his studies than his administrative achievements.

In the Leewards Christopher III, like his father, was forced to tackle at an early age, the complex problems of corruption and inefficiency in the Government, coupled with a widespread breakdown of law. He reacted with energy and skill. Pere Labat, (one of the few contemporary diarists) who met him at St. Kitts in 1701 remarks that he was full of sharp questions and much more sober than most Englishmen. Judgement-day for feather-nested officials was at hand.

Of a corrupt Customs Commissioner on Nevis, Codrington reported to the Board of Trade:

> he had been more absolute in Nevis before my arivall than any Bashaw was, and thinks it a great encroachment upon his antient privileges to be within the reach of law and justice.

Of a notorious Mr. Norton who had bought his Lieutenant-Governorship on St. Christophers in order to exploit his powers, Codrington reported "it would be impossible to put the poor ruined people of that island with any tolerable order whilst he continued at their head". Norton had acted like a gangster, using all kinds of bully-boy tactics to extort money, evict tenants, imprison and terrorise.

At one point he had browbeaten George Lennard, the inoffensive Governor of the little island of Anguilla into signing an indenture of servitude. "After which", wrote Codrington, "he was forced to work in the fields as a slave, almost naked and half-starved. Once or twice a week Colonel Norton caused him to be whipped in the pillory and the pickle of beef brine to be put on his sores." The new Governor-General was unable to prescribe the same medicine to the bully, but he was suspended in disgrace and bought a new plantation where he was less well known.

What Codrington tried to do could only destroy him. He tried to apply the letter of the law to people who had learnt to ignore it because it conflicted with their own view of their best interests. The men of the law, as well as almost all officials, were corruptible, beyond anything comparable in England. Codrington had not the experience to know it, he could not cope with it, and the frusration made him ill.

> The disorder in our Trade is so great, that I almost despair of going any good in it, there is much ignorance, laziness or corruption in Naval and

31

Customhouse officers, and so general a conspiracy in people of all ranks and qualitys here to elude the Acts of Trade.

Finally, in the act of mounting a successful attack on the French island of Guadeloupe, he became very ill and asked to be relieved. Succeeded by a quick succession of total nincompoops who undid his good work in a fraction of the time it had taken to achieve, Codrington retired to his estates on Barbados where he died, a broken man, aged 42.

Before he had left England, he had bought the old family estate at Dodington with its great Elizabethan house and ordered improvements to enable him to retire there in grand style. Christopher had no heir, so, on his death, the greater part of his vast fortune and West Indian estates, together with Dodington Hall, went to his nephew William.

Before he died, however, he made two other bequests. He gave his enormous book collection to Oxford, leaving All Souls enough money to build a magnificent library around it and maintain it. To the newly-formed Society for the Propagation of the Gospel, he left his Barbados estates and slaves, to be used in the foundation of a new educational college "to maintain a convenient number of Professors and Scholars" and medical missionaries from the proceeds of sugar. Controversy surrounded the project from the beginning. The S.P.G. were sure that Codrington had intended the bequest to be used for the Christianisation of negro slaves — the Barbadians were equally sure it was for the schooling of white children, and nephew William thought the idea was a Papist plot and contested the Will. When this was eventually settled in favour of the S.P.G., the plantations had suffered from neglect. They never became the showcase for gentle Christian principles which was Codrington's wish and the happy dream of metropolitan Bishops, but by the 19th century a decent imposing sort of establishment had grown up, with genuinely multi-racial freedoms, from which generations of free West Indians emerged to take up posts in teaching, administration or politics.

In 1721 William received a Baronetcy as a sort of recognition for the family's services to the Crown. He went on to become an M.P. and held various seats for 45 years, voting with the West Indian group on issues which concerned him personally, otherwise he was a typical country gentleman. In all that time he is known to have made only one speech and that on a game bill. There have been Codringtons at Dodington until modern times and the present incumbent has opened the house to the public. The men have maintained a steady military tradition, fighting with distinction in either army or navy. There have been two Admirals and three Generals, all of whom played a part in the making of the British Empire in its second phase of expansion.

Capability Brown superbly re-designed the park for William in the mid-century and his first cousin and successor Christopher Bethell Codrington had James Wyatt rebuild the house on a lavish and grand scale. The imposing pillared portico of Roman inspiration was no doubt a tribute to the Codringtons' image of themselves as Imperial Consuls Extraordinary.

In the wake of the Civil War, James Drax and twelve other Barbadian planters were knighted by Charles II for their loyalty and sacrifice during the recent troubles. King Charles was quite aware that Barbados was indeed his "most precious Jewel", but the problem was how to take a very substantially larger part of the profits than the Crown received from its customs duties and proprietorial rents. One way was to create a Royal monopoly in the slave trade. The Royal African Company was founded to set up trading stations on the West African coast, to trade for slaves and ship them to the Indies. The Duke of York, the King's brother, was in charge. It worked badly from the very start. It overcharged the planters, it was inefficient, it was always behind with its deliveries, and never had enough slaves to satisfy demand. The independent-minded planters worked with the Company's agents as far as possible, but smuggled slaves when they could. It was a game that all the most important personages on Barbados played. The factors complained to the King. One wrote:

> Unless the King support the Company and discountenance those in places of trust who ought to support his rights, but instead thereof not only are breakers themselves but encourage others, we shall never see the Company established in full enjoyment of its grant. Colonel Henry Drax and Mr. John Peers of the Council of Barbados are such men, and also we are informed, Colonel Christopher Codrington, Lt. Col. John Codrington and Mr. Samuel Husbands . . . Two interlopers have lately landed their negroes at the usual point to leeward; one carried 90, the other 110. We could not prevent it . . .

The King tried other measures, amongst them the appointment of outsiders who were nominees of his own to official posts on the island. These posts were ill-paid, but the customary fees and other emoluments more than made up for that. Outsiders had no compunction at all in increasing these fees, often quite arbitrarily. Further, it became customary for the owner of these places to absent themselves from Barbados altogether and to rent the place profitably to another who was either prepared to sail to the West Indies or may have already been there in some junior position. Such measures caused ill will and eventually administrative chaos. In the third quarter of the century many of the biggest planters left Barbados for good and returned to England. Others waited until the Revolution in 1688 and then pinned their hopes on petitioning the new King for reforms. Many of them too, realised that they had gone too far. The island was now grossly over-crowded and the tension between the small, thinly spread number of whites and the large number of brutalised negro slave gangs was nerve-wracking. Food was always a serious problem and even more so when His Majesty in London decided to play with the shipping life-line. Further, there were clear indications of soil exhaustion and profits might be more difficult in future.

There was already a substantial group of planters who had settled in London and become sugar merchants or commission agents for the colony. Now others joined them, bought land in the country and took an active part in political life.

These planters were enormously rich; they were responsible for a large slice of England's overseas trade; they had been trained in a hard and corrupt school; they were indeed men to reckon with, hard and ambitious enough to make their way in the capital. John Colleton, Edward Littleton, the planters most eloquent pamphleteers, and the Drax's, all left and settled in England for good. Henry Drax bought an estate in Dorset and virtually con-trolled the Wareham constituency. Thomas Earle Drax sat for both Corfe Castle and Wareham in the mid 18th century. By shrewd marriages they moved steadily into the labyrinthine networks of the gentry, which was increasingly reflected in *their* interests and occupations — sheriffs and J.P's, career military men and large scale farmers. Today, Drax is still a powerful name in Dorset and around Richmond Yorkshire, where the family have another large estate. One branch of the Drax's married into the Irish gentry and the menfolk became the Barons of Dunsany. Edward Drax, the 18th Baron was a well-known Edwardian author and play-wright who flickered about the circle of Lady Gregory and the Abbey Theatre, Dublin. The Dorset Drax's have commingled with Plunketts and Ernles and became Plunkett-Ernle-Erle-Drax by Royal License. The late head of the family, Reginald Aylmer Plunkett-Ernle-Erle-Drax, was in the Navy, spending part of the 1930's as Commander-in-Chief on the West India station. His son and heir also made the Navy his life and retired as an Admiral.

The Master Planters

These men and women created a new kind of society in the West Indies, announced their intention of making a fortune and then retired to England to enjoy it. A great number died in the attempt, a few failed, but the rest created, for a brief generation or two, a breed of master-planter who dominated all around it. In Barbados, they created the British colonial version of the sugar plantation, introduced and developed sugar and slaves into a hugely profitable industry which engaged the whole country with its trade, its wars, and finally its morality.

Sugar-cane ... has such a benign faculty, as to preserve all the rest from corruption, which without it, would taint and become rotten.

(Richard Ligon 1657)

4

An 18th Century Godfather

A few months after the triumphant Restoration of Charles II in 1660, Samuel Pepys, Secretary to the Navy, received a visitor in his room at the Admiralty. "The great Tom Fuller came to me to desire a kindness for a friend of his who hath a mind to go to Jamaica." The friend was Peter Beckford, a young man of good family, but of no fortune. The event, scarcely interesting at the time, was nevertheless noted in the famous diary and provides us today with our first recorded glimpse of the founder of the Beckford fortune on his way.

Jamaica was England's newest colony, a dangerous and deadly frontier, riddled with disease and threatened by Spanish and Maroon (freed black slaves) guerillas. In 1655 Cromwell's expeditionary force — the spearhead of a Grand Design for building a new Republican Colonial Empire on the broken back of the Spanish West — failed in their first task of taking San Domingo on the island of Hispaniola and decided to try their luck on neighbouring Jamaica instead. Here, more fortunately, the Spaniards decamped, scattering their cattle and horses to the wild open spaces and freeing their negro slaves to organise resistance in the hills. "God seemed to smile" on the Protestant English, the expedition got ashore and took possession. Penn and Venables, the two commanders, were incompetent and at odds with each other; the troops were weakly and indisciplined, the planters recruited in Barbados were "the most debauched . . . Scorners of Religion". Reinforcements and supplies failed to arrive — instead of food, the Government sent Bibles. Yet, despite the terrible toll of life from fever rather than foe, the colony was somehow secured and the guerillas damped down. Charles II had promised to return Jamaica to the Spanish King in return for help in regaining his own throne,

36

but as the Restoration was achieved without Spanish assistance, he felt only the merest pang of conscience in breaking his promise. Jamaica was without any doubt an important conquest, potentially profitable, large enough to swallow ten Barbados, and everyone knew that Barbados even now was "the principal pearl in his Majesty's Crown".

What exactly motivated the young Beckford to go to Jamaica is not known. Such information as trickled back from the island cannot have been reassuring: starvation, martial law, a mutinous and unpaid army wishing to leave as quickly as possible, a rabble of would-be planters chaffing under military discipline, a hinterland alive with marauding bands of negro slaves released by the Spaniards when they left, and in the ports gangs of pirates for whom the island was a perfect base. Land-a-plenty was the main lure; a chance for the small planter which was denied on the overcrowded over-planted islands of Barbados and St. Kitts.

Attitudes to emigration had changed radically since the early years of colonial expansion. England was now held to be short of people; she could not afford to send her citizens off into the blue unless there was a good commercial reason. Sending men and women to Massachusetts which produced no commodity England needed, was seen as a waste. Sending emigrants to the Indies which produced tropical commodities the home country could not produce, but could sell, was a different matter. Better still if those goods were to be shipped only in English bottoms to English ports. Top marks if one emigrant Englishman in charge of a gang of black slaves or poor whites multiplied the fruits of his labour ten or even a hundred times. That was high commercial good sense. There was little loss to the home country and there were many more bodies to feed and clothe with English goods which in turn would require more English ships. This was the cornerstone of the mercantilist philosophy.

There were two sailing routes to Jamaica, the first from London to New England and down the American Eastern seaboard, slipping between Cuba and Hispaniola directly to Jamaica, or to sail down the African coast to catch the Trade Winds to Barbados and then on to Jamaica. The former held the greater risk of meeting with privateers and other hostile ships amongst the Bahamas and around the large Spanish islands — no problem for a convoy or a fleet, but always dangerous for single ships. The more usual route, especially after the English fleet came effectively to dominate the whole of the Western seaboard of Europe from the Channel to the Canary Islands and beyond, was to take the Barbados route which was shorter. Barbados was an important trading centre in its own right and profitable business could always be done there.

Not having the capital to buy a plantation, Beckford launched the family fortune by turning horse catcher. A successful one could make a lot of money. The Spaniards in 1655, pursuing a primitive kind of burnt earth policy, scattered their flocks of sheep, herds of cattle and horses into the woods as they withdrew. For five years the hungry English had hunted and killed for food, but Jamaica being a big island, the risks of venturing out of known friendly territory were high. Horses were difficult to ship and were consequently precious. "This afforded an occasion to a good many of those," writes an early historian of Jamaica, "who are now prouder than our Dukes and Marquesses, to so make a livelihood of, and to lay the foundation of the estates they now enjoy." Beckford was quite prepared to take the necessary risks for the sake of the quick return, and while many perished, he prospered, with capital to enter into business *and* start building up a plantation.

As the military threat faded, Jamaica began to enjoy the atmosphere of a gold rush, a disorderly, greedy and above all thirsty scrummage attracting the riff-raff of the ocean and disillusioned or debauched from the older colonies. For much of the century, pirates and privateers were welcome, their prize money and their pay poured into the taverns and bordellos of Port Royal and many a merchant made a killing. Beckford was one of them, building an interest as a wine merchant, shipping and selling wine to an almost insatiable market.

One of the earliest Governors of Jamaica was Sir Thomas Modyford, an ambitious pioneer planter from Barbados. Son of a mayor of Exeter and a convinced Royalist, he had fled to Barbados in the losing moments of the Civil War, taking with him both money and connections. There he prospered and played a leading part in island politics, becoming Governor, despite his sympathies, in the last year of the Commonwealth. For this he spent several years in the political wilderness before influence and friends commended him sufficiently to the new King and he was offered the challenging, prickly post in Jamaica. Selling off his Barbadian property, he set about building a new and much more profitable personal empire for himself and his family, giving himself patents for a vast acreage of prime land on which he developed a huge sugar plantation with an army of slaves. At the same time, there was no conflict in his mind to promote the cause of the small planter. At last, in Jamaica, he felt there was room for the small man, the grant of land to indentured servants at the end of their term, a yeomanry of planters in fact. He urged the King to be prodigal in granting the first million acres and to offer tax concessions to would-be immigrants. In seven years in fact Modyford issued over 1800 land patents, mostly in the fertile areas of the south coast within a day or so's riding from the administrative capital at Spanish Town.

Beckford began to plant at this time in the parish of St. Catherines which contained Spanish Town and Beckford's own town mansion. By the end of his life his estates ran into thousands of acres. Against the acre to acre solidarity of the Beckfords, the Modyfords and their like, the yeoman planter could hardly survive. The big capitalists had all the advantages. Growing sugar was big business. The most economical method of production was on big plantations with large slave gangs. Slaves and land together were more than the small man could afford and he was unable to compete. By the end of the century, Jamaica too was being run in the interests of a small elite of large planters, owning huge estates manned by armies of slaves.

From horse rustling, to wine, to sugar growing, Beckford accumulated power and capital without pause. He was ruthless and irascible — "one of the great incendiaries here", complained one of the Governors to London, but at the same time he was extremely successful both in business and administration. By the end of his life he had held almost all the top offices in the colony including a short spell as Acting Governor when the incumbent died. As Colonel of Militia and Commander and Custos of Port Royal, he is portrayed in 1692 glaring belligerently at us from the canvas, his hand resting lightly on his sword which we know he drew at the slightest provocation. He is wearing the most elaborate brocaded coat covered in gold leaf, a huge feathered hat lies on the table beside him. He poses like a conquering hero, his face, even through the flattering brush of a hack portraitist, a mask of dogmatism and pugnacity. Over his shoulder through an open window is a distant landscape of coastline prominently featuring a squat fort flying the British flag.

The irony of appearing as a loyal and energetic commander was undoubtedly lost on Beckford. The uniform was the thing. In fact, Beckford was a firebrand leading planter in opposition to the levy of revenue used to finance defence. The Assembly — in effect the planters parliament spent the greater part of its time wrangling over ways to delay due payments. The English regiments and naval flotilla based on Jamaica suffered accordingly. Admiral Benbow, faced with Beckford and his fellows, wrote home to the Secretary of State Vernon:

The Government of this Island now is entirely in the hands of Planters who mind nothing but getting Estates and when so to goe off, having no regard to the King's Interest or Subjects, for at this time we can hardly get fresh Provisions to Support the Sick, the Ships and Soldiers being a great burthen to them as they say and wish they had never come into these parts. The Inhabitants are grown very rich and value themselves for being Judges and Parties in making and executing their own Laws; they doe whatever they desire of Gain leads them to without any regard to the Laws of our Country.

The Assembly was seldom a place of quiet law-making. Beckford's most usual method of speeding up debate was to hit his colleagues on the head with a large stick he carried for the purpose. Understandably he was not always popular. "I have gone through most of the offices of this island, though with no great applause, yet without complaint," he wrote in an unusual fit of modesty.

Characteristically, it was in a bitter wrangle over revenue that he died in 1710. His son Peter, who that year was Speaker of the Assembly, found himself pinned at sword-point, while members of the House attempted to pass measures with which he disagreed. His father, elderly and retired, but choleric as usual, attempted to interfere but fell in a scuffle and never recovered.

Peter married twice; the first lady died without issue, but by the second there were three sons and two daughters. The eldest, also called Peter, inherited the bulk of his father's estate and continued to build successfully on it. Son Charles died in infancy, Thomas died in a fight when still a young man, but left a widow and a son. Two daughters married well and started their own spheres of influence. The Beckford dynasty was on the move.

Meanwhile, England and indeed all of Europe, were demanding more and more sugar. First chocolate, then coffee and later tea became popular everyday drinks. In Queen Elizabeth's time scarcely one pound of sugar per person per year was the average consumption, and most of that amongst the wealthy. By the reign of James II it was four pounds a head and by 1720 eight pounds. Sugar supplied molasses for distillation into rum. Sugar went into medicine, into jams, and revolutionised cake making. Apothecaries recommended treacle as a powerful specific for all poisons. Because of treacle, gingerbread could be made and parkin be covetted by good North country lads and lasses.

From the 1720's Jamaica's sugar exports consistently exceeded those of Barbados. Sugar was the subject of endless economic tracts and treatises. In short, sugar for the 18th century economy held the place that steel occupied in the 19th and oil in the 20th, writes Eric Williams in his masterly survey of West Indian economic history, "Capitalism and Slavery". Sugar and King.

The change-over to the Hanoverian Kings in 1714 made little difference in the Caribbean. The pursuit of profit went on as fast as ever. The pioneering days were far behind and the sugar barons aspired to a more refined style of life, building Great Houses — copies of Palladian mansions seen in England and furnished with à la mode hangings and carpets. They equipped coaches and kept fine horses. They trained black huntsmen and pursued wild hogs. They entertained on a lavish scale and cultivated all the fashionable and gentlemanly leisure pursuits such as horse-racing, fishing, gambling, cards and backgammon, assemblies and balls. No-one however, was deluded into believing these entertainments came near to the delights available in London, the metropolis, or the houses of the more comfortable English gentry. Most of the time life was dull, society boorish, the men barbarous and the servants dirty and disobedient.

The difficulty with so many of these 17th and 18th century families is that the names remain the same through several generations, so in the Beckford family, Peter, William and Richard occur repeatedly to the great confusion of the writer and, necessarily, also the reader. Short of inventing nicknames there is no alternative but to consider them a dynasty and number them, I, II etc. as they appear.

Of Peter II there are no anecdotes to relate. He was a true "Creole". That is, he was born and lived his life on Jamaica taking part fully in its society and sharing its prejudices. He was a long married, mature, some would say a middle-aged man, when his father died. His sisters had married well, one of them to George Ellis, a member of another of Jamaica's leading planter families who became a Chief Justice — a useful alliance, with extensive plantations of his own, active in island politics and holding in addition the lucrative post of Comptroller of Her Majesty's Customs during the reign of Queen Anne. If the size of his family means anything, he must have liked and been proud of his children, for his wife Bathsua bore him thirteen, both sons and daughters, and he sent the surviving sons to Westminster, from which school they naturally went on to University. The Jamaican estates were expanded both by purchase and by taking up new grants. Though one has to treat reported figures with caution, he certainly appears at the time of his death, to have been the wealthiest planter in Jamaica. Official records show that he held in his own name over 3,500 acres and that he was sole owner of nine sugar plantations and part-owner of seven more. He had nine cattle pens, several farms, and a palatial house in Spanish Town. He owned 1737 slaves and half-owned another 577. His total personal property amounted to £233,314 with another £100,000 or so in building. Another £20,000 was written in for his personal property in England, "besides diverse large Quantities of Sugar and other Merchandise", consigned to Thomas Beckford, his cousin and London commission agent.

Few placed any value on formal education in Jamaica. Charles Leslie, an early historian wrote in 1740:

> Learning is here at Lowest Ebb; there is no Publick School in the whole Island, neither do they seem fond of the Thing: several large Donations have been made for such Uses but have never taken Effect. The office of a Teacher is look'd upon as contemptible, and no Gentleman keeps Company with one of that Character; to read, write and cost up Accounts, is all the Education they desire, and even those are but scurvily taught. A man of any parts or Learning that would employ himself in that business would be despised and starve. The Gentlemen, whose Fortunes can allow, send their Children to Great Britain, where they have the Advantage of a polite generous Education, but others are spoil'd, and make such an inconsiderable figure ever after, that they are the common Butt in every Conversation. . .

The lack of schools was both cause and effect of counter-migration back to England. Planters who counted on spending a few years only in the colony would not be bothered; those who expected to stay could not be prevailed upon to combine with their fellows. It was the same with all affairs of common concern and benefit such as roads or bridges; canals, dams or defence. So the absence of schools was the first great step in encouraging absenteeism. It was the eldest son and heir who received the priority treatment and was shipped off to England first — the careers of West Indian families show how few returned. They preferred to live the comfortable easy life to which their education had accustomed them, squeezing every advantage from their allowances and waiting for the family fortune to fall into their lap.

Nevertheless Peter II felt it necessary to conform to custom. As soon as they approached the age of thirteen, Peter II shipped his boys back to England to be educated and, money being no object, there was no difficulty in entering them into Westminster where they could be expected at least to learn the virtues of discipline by terror, pick up a little Latin or Greek, but above all, to make friends and useful connections amongst gentlemen's sons.

Money certainly opened the door to the possibility of social acceptance in English 18th century high society, but it did not by itself ensure it. Young West Indian masters arrived in England with heavy disabilities. Their sallow complexions stood out. Left largely to the care and supervision of negro servants from babyhood, they had picked up a sing-song accent barely understandable as English. Their book-learning was well behind and they faced the humiliation of sitting with much younger boys until they could catch up. Their parents' wealth combined with exaggerated visions of their future fortunes, made them the natural bait for all kinds of financial rapacity. The Beckford boys overcame most of these handicaps, though William was never to lose the accent. Westminster led to Oxford, where dining, drinking and riding were the main pursuits. . .

> and he was sent home like a well-threshed ear of corn, with nothing in his head: having finished his education to the high satisfaction of the master and fellows of his college, who had, in testimony of their approbation, presented him with a silver fish-slice, on which his name figured at the head of a laudatory inscription in some semi-barbarous dialect of Anglo-Saxonised Latin.
>
> (Nightmare Abbey. Thomas Love Peacock)

The normal circuit of the elder son in the 17th century was completed when he returned from University to help his father run his estate or his business, but after 1700 a new fad had spread through the upper classes — the Grand Tour, a high style travel tour through France and Italy by the means of which the uncouth Northerner was able to absorb the culture and elegance of the ancient world. And those who would cut a dash sent home, not postcards of Capri or the Colisseum, but packing cases of paintings, porcelain and miscellaneous Roman bric-a-brac.

The early adult life of the Beckford boys in England is lost in obscurity. Certainly William moved from Oxford to Leyden University in Holland where he enrolled as a medical student, though there is no evidence that he intended to practice or showed any interest in medical matters during the rest of his life. From there he must have travelled, for he became an omniverous, though not always discriminating, collector of objets d'art with which he stuffed his various homes. The likelihood is that he then entered one of the London businesses such as cousin Thomas Beckford's Commission House dealing with West Indian trade, in which his father had an interest. The City soon became his fundamental interest. He is known to have returned to Jamaica once at the time of his father's death, which made him the richest if not the most powerful planter in Jamaica. He chose, however, to treat his Jamaican properties as his own personal gold mines and quickly returned to England where he could exercise more power and influence. Absenteeism was to him a way of life, for he wrote:

> the climate of our sugar colonies is so inconvenient for an English constitution that no man will choose to live there, much less will any man choose to settle there, without the hopes at least of supporting his family in a more handsome manner, or saving more money, than he can do by any business he can expect in England, or in our plantations upon the continent of America.

Richard and Julines both inherited Jamaican estates and became important planters in their own right. Both of them spent time in Jamaica looking after the family interests and combined this with an active City life. Julines however, married into the squirarchy and acquired estates at Steepleton Iwerne and Shillingstone in Dorset, from which have sprung several generations of wealthy, charming and slightly dotty country gentlemen. His son Peter was sent to Westminster and Oxford where hunting seems to have taken a firm grip. Although he entered politics briefly, it was hunting which really interested him and he became the first English writer to describe accurately the whole system of the sport. "Never", wrote a contemporary wit "had fox or hare the honour of being chased to death by so accomplished a hunter; never was a huntsman's dinner graced by such urbanity and wit. He would bag a fox in Greek, find a hare in Latin, inspect his kennels in Italian, and direct the economy of his stables in exquisite French."

He inherited his father's Jamaican estates, which were in excess of 8,000 acres, but was content to leave them with an agent and collect the revenue. His father-in-law was "randy" George Pitt, whose see-saw political fortunes were finally rewarded with a new Barony of Lord Rivers of Strathfield Saye, the ancestral Pitt Estate. Daughter Elizabeth married the second Earl of Effingham, while the elder son Francis married Albina Bertie, daughter of the Duke of Ancaster. William Horace Beckford, the surviving son of hunting Peter, succeeded to the Rivers title in 1828 and changed his name from Beckford to Pitt-Rivers. The family has continued to this day to manage large estates in Dorset and Wiltshire. One of them, the late Victorian General Pitt-Rivers was a brilliant amateur archaeologist who excavated burial mounds all over Dorset and left meticulous and elaborate models of the work, together with a huge and heterogeneous collection of

ancient and primitive art amassed during his campaigns or safaris throughout the British Empire. He also laid out some elegant and rather bizarre gardens known as the Larner Grounds which were open to the public.

Brother Richard is soon dealt with. After Balliol, he entered the Inner Temple, one of the few recognised training grounds where knowledge of the law of contracts and similar useful aids to the management of a complex trading company could be learned. He then opted for a City career, combining personal care of his estates in Jamaica with assiduous though modest attention to the Liveried Company of Goldsmiths through which he became an Alderman two years before his early death in 1756. He never married and his estates, amounting to 9,242 acres, devolved on his other brothers.

William Beckford was a man difficult to fit into any neat category, a private man who lived and revelled in the public; a complex and contradictory character, a figure the media today would have loved. His love of women and the good things of life, his brood of much cherished illegitimate children; his swaggering mansions stuffed with plunder; his fleet of ships; his armies of slaves; his power in the City; his funny voice; his partiality for political sensationalism — they were the stuff of headlines and lawsuits and general outrage. William Beckford did not have to struggle to attain his financial power; it fell into his hands by inheritance from his older brother and his father who died within a short time of each other, leaving him the master of huge combined sugar plantations, factoring and shipping companies. These together formed the most powerful single economic interest in Jamaica with tentacles throughout the West Indies, the American colonies, and of course in London. London was where William wished to be, it was the only place where he could make proper use of the riches he had accumulated and it was also where all the decisions were made affecting colonial trade. It was where the news of new markets first circulated; it was the seat of Imperial government, a place on which a young and energetic colonial millionaire might legitimately set his heart.

So Beckford moved the headquarters of the family business to England where he continued to build up the family fortune. His active business life coincided with a wave of prosperity for the sugar industry. The deliberate throttling of French and Spanish competition by the all-powerful and belligerent British Navy during the Seven Years War (1756-1763) meant that Europe was temporarily starved of alternative supplies. To the monopoly of the British market, which the West Indies already possessed, was added a surging export business. Demand exceeded supply and the price of raw sugar rose rapidly. An avalanche of surplus capital poured into the planters' pockets giving many besides Beckford the opportunity "to shine in the mother-country". It was not easy for the colonial to enter English society at the level he felt he deserved. Beckford was richer than most of the English peerage and owned a larger acreage than most Dukes. But it was land-ownership in England that gave a man "bottom", as solid worth was called, and it was membership of the right families which gave one entree into high society.

England in the greater part of the 18th century was dominated by a tight, self-perpetuating peerage of some 200 persons forming a network of powerful, rich cousineages under the patronage of the ducal heads of great Whig families – Russells, Cavendishes, Fitzwilliams, Pelhams and so forth. They functioned as families, more like giant stock companies today. At regular board meetings – traditionally the opening of the shooting season or a patriarchal birthday celebration, alliances were formulated and marriages arranged as social and economic contracts designed to protect private property and the continuance of the male line. The rich outsider could aspire to social advancement and was often success-ful. Charles II after all, had created thirteen Baronetcies in Barbados soon after the Restoration. Rich planters who served as island Governors were frequently knighted and rich city merchants had been honoured for lending money to the always needy Crown. Marriage with the daughter of a penniless peer was often a good proposition. There were more ways than one of arriving. The foresighted sent their sons to public schools or bought them army commissions in both of which "interest" or connection might be assured. More often than not, however, the nouveau-riche went about it the wrong way, expecting to be able somehow to shoulder his way through. He built a huge house in imitation of the gentry, he cultivated a taste for country sports, he overdressed his wife and daughters and retained an extravagent troupe of liveried servants with which he travelled about, all of which labelled him as an upstart.

Beckford went about it systematically, though not always wisely. Part of the new income went back into the Jamaican estates and to acquiring new ones. It must have been at about this time that he acquired new grants of land in Westmoreland, the most westerly of all Jamaican parishes and bought many new slaves to work it. The record shows that William increased his slave force from 691 in 1735 to 1,093 in 1774. More of his capital went into developing his shipping, factoring and commission business. He lent money to other Jamaican planters and he underwrote loans to the Government.

He wanted to have a voice in City politics so he had himself adopted by the Company of Ironmongers, from which he was duly adopted as an Alderman. In 1755 he was made Sheriff, during which year, he is said to have performed his civic functions admirably and to have given four great banquets at his own charge. In 1762 he became a notable Lord Mayor and was again Lord Mayor in 1769, dying during his year of office. The Lord Mayor's last great dinner before he died offered a choice of 600 dishes served on gold plate, at a cost of over £10,000. "The splendour of which," it was reported, "eclipsed anything of the kind prepared in the City within human memory, and never since approached." These were not his only official city functions either, for he fancied himself in uniform as well, holding the title of Colonel in the City's White Regiment for eight years and the Treasurership of the Honourable Artillery Company in the last year of his life. All of this, however, was undoubtedly a form of compensation for the "cold shouldering" he got from the gentry. At least while William was alive his many businesses flourished. He understood the pitfalls of controlling plantations at such a distance and he maintained a firm, even tyrannical line, with his agents and overseers on the spot. This ensured that the returns were satisfactory, but it undoubtedly led to the increased exploitation of the slave labour force and to the greater use of brutal punishment as the managers strove to meet their targets. It was such brutal treatment which led to a large scale slave uprising in 1760 led by a Koromantee slave on one of the Beckford estates. There was a great deal of bloodshed and arson, both during the rising and as a result of its suppression. Some 60 Europeans lost their lives and over 400 slaves. The ring leader was captured and burnt alive. Two of his lieutenants were hung up to dry in irons, a fourth was condemned to have his legs slowly burnt off. Such punishment was considered necessary to protect the rapidly shrinking population of masters against the rapidly rising population of slaves.

Shortly after his return from Jamaica in 1736, William bought a huge estate of some four to five thousand acres at Fonthill in Wiltshire, together with a solid 17th century house which in its turn had replaced an Elizabethan manor. It was a purchase which might well be considered to confer social prestige. But if the new squire expected to be adopted by the traditional country gentry, he was disappointed. To them, Beckford was a radical nouveau riche, and even in the tolerant atmosphere of the period, his morals shocked them. Certainly Beckford never sought to hide his "amorous propensities". He did not marry until 1760 and in the

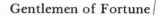

meantime he entertained his ladies in the great house just as if he was in Jamaica where it was quite the done thing. He adored his natural children and his eldest, and favourite, Richard, lived with him at Fonthill until he married. He became a partner in several of his father's factoring houses and showed flair for trade, living to be a terrible thorn in the side for young William, the legitimate son and heir, and a Trojan Horse in the family business empire. There were numerous other boys and girls, for all of whom he found situations or arranged comfortable marriages.

Thwarted in his sincere but naive attempts to found a "county family", spurned by the gentry, Beckford entered politics. It was a natural step, though it was not in the nature of the man to plan his way forward with any great precision. It was almost certainly an impulsive urge for which there were excellent reasons.

Firstly money. Access to the most lucrative Government contracts and the privilege of offering to loan the Government money was only given to merchants or bankers who were members of the House of Commons. They were the reward of the obedient and the profits were gigantic. Social advancements might also follow with a Baronetcy becoming "the crest over the profits", as one historian puts it. The second reason was that it was expected of him. A man of his standing needed to be in the Commons. Thirdly, he could more effectively lead the group protecting and furthering the West India Interest from inside the House of Commons than outside it. Fourthly, because the House of Commons was not just the best coffee house in London where agreeable conversation was to be had, but it was also the best theatre, a place of instant drama. There was a side of Beckford's character, inherited perhaps from his grandfather, which often forced him to show off, to posture and rant. Politics became a kind of lightning conductor through which he discharged a great deal of his restless energy.

He quickly alligned himself in the cause of Pitt the Elder and followed his star through thick and thin for the rest of his life. He spoke frequently in the House and Chatham welcomed his support there, but he was a bad-speaker, and was often too self-absorbed to be effective in debate. His contemporaries judged him particularly harshly. The famous blue-stocking, Mrs. Montagu, said he was one "whom no arguement can convince, no defeat make ashamed, nor mistake make diffident". Horace Walpole called him "a noisy vapouring fool". Nevertheless he was by no means a negligible political figure. He was a great electioneer, masterminding elections for his brothers while running his own in a different part of the country. He persuaded many members of his family and their West Indian planter friends who had till then shown little interest in politics, to follow him into the Commons and he thus created a powerful pressure group — a Cousinhood which when the occasion arose acted and voted like one man in what it saw as its best commercial interest. The Government of the moment ignored it at its peril.

A group of merchants in the City who were no doubt being encouraged by the Government to find seats so that they might have a contract or two complained in 1754 that absentees were able to:

> support contests in some of the richest and most populous cities in this Country. No less than three brothers from one of our sugar islands having offered themselves, one for London, one for Bristol, and one for Salisbury; and a fourth brother, according to what has been published in the publick papers, intended for a Wiltshire Borough.

The West Indians were in fact pushing up the price of rotten Boroughs and seizing them from under the noses of fat cats in the City who were thus prevented from qualifying for their contracts. And not only the merchants were affected. Lord Chesterfield, seeking to buy a seat for his son in 1767 received a gruff reply from a borough-monger: "he laughed at my offer, and said, that there was no such thing as a borough to be had now; for that the rich East and West Indians had secured them all, at the rate of three thousand pounds at least; but many at four thousand; and two or three, that he knew, at five thousand".

That touchstone of well informed men-about-town "The Gentlemans Magazine" in one of its 1766 issues carried a piece about colonial trade in which the author wrote:

> If I am not mis-informed, there are now in Parliament upwards of forty Members who are either West Indian planters themselves, descended from such, or have concerns there than entitle them to this pre-iminence.

No-one could deny in the mid-years of the 18th century that the West Indies were the richest British colonies, that they gave work to thousands of men and women throughout the United Kingdom, or that they oiled the wheels of the rapidly developing financial broking and banking business, or that they were the lifeblood of the merchant navy — the argument was developed frequently in numerous pamphlets and petitions of the time. But there was something disquieting about this "foreign" invasion of "Creoles", all of them as bold as brass and stinking rich, whose self-confessed and only purpose in entering Parliament was to make damned sure they got even richer, quicker than before.

Gentlemen of Fortune

The core of the cousinship was the Beckford family, the leader of which was Alderman William then brother Richard and Julines. There were then the Pennants, the Dawkins and the Morants, all cousins of the Beckfords and very big planters in their own right. Another cousin, Ithamar Vassall married Rose Fuller, who sat at various times for New Romney and Maidstone and whose brother Stephen was official agent for the Jamaican planters' interests for thirty years. Ithamar's brother Florentius Vassall married a sister of Thomas Foster, another planter who represented Cornish and Dorset constituencies, and another of Foster's sisters married William Matthew Burt, a St. Kitts planter. A. L. Swymmer, who sat for Southampton from 1747, was a cousin of Rose Fuller, and thus distantly related to the Beckfords. He was joined at Southampton by Hans Stanley, a cousin of his and when Swymmer died, Henry Dawkins came in with the Fuller's support. This was just the caucus, but there were the planters from other islands. James Colleton and Sir John Gibbons from Barbados, together with veteran absentee planters Thomas Earle Drax and Sir William Codrington, three members of the Lascelles family including the future first Earl of Harewood. Sir James Lowther, son of an ex-Governor and Fane William Sharpe. From Grenada there was John Thomlinson, both a planter and a prominent City merchant; from Nevis, William Woodley and from Antigua, Samual Martin.

These were the actual fighters, the actual muscle men who went in the political ring and slugged it out when the glove was down, but outside the ring there were many others who, if I can continue the analogy, were the seconds, the fight managers, the publicists even the retired fighters who had gone into managements. All these too were part of what was called The West India Interest and during its heyday, limited to the Beckford Cousinhood. There were the agents of the resident planters whose interests in some cases conflicted with the absentees. There were growing numbers of absentee planters, widows and families of planters living in Marylebone and Bath; there were the holders of sinecures and other official gifts who had chosen to rent out their appointments at a profitable fee rather than risk the sea journey and discomfort of a sojourn in the Indies; there were the shippers, the insurers and the factors who provided long-term credit at high risk but high profitability also; the wool and linen merchants and all the other tradesmen who supplied the sugar and the slave trade. All of these were part of it, or could be relied upon to create a clamour should the occasion arise. There were opulent dinners to flatter Ministers and shape opinion, there were pamphlets and petitions to prepare and print, M.P's to canvas and civil servants to wait upon. The outposts of Bristol, Liverpool, Whitehaven and Glasgow, to name only the main centres of trade with the colonies, were deeply concerned with all matters of trade, customs duties and shipping restrictions.

In a House of some 550 members divided by issues and principles into major political parties or groupings, a caucus of forty or so individuals, whose major concern was one aspect only of the Nation's commercial life, would not necessarily have caused a strong Government too much concern. But mid-18th century Parliamentary politics were the faction fights of men more apt to weigh the obligation created, or the price which could be asked for each and every vote. These factions were like scurrying blobs of mercury on a plate tilted from side to side, ceaselessly splitting and reforming, at times attracted to the biggest blob, at other times fragmented into dozens of tiny globules. In such an activity, a faction of forty or so members would be a largish blob capable of attracting its own globules and even of tipping the balance in its favour.

In 1733, even before the Beckfords came on the scene, the sugar interest had pushed through a Molasses Act which attempted to restrict, by heavy taxation, the import of foreign sugar, molasses and rum into the mainland American colonies — a blow aimed at the French sugar colonies which also embittered the Americans. The Americans, who had no similar caucus in the House, railed against "the iniquitous schemes of these overgrown West Indians", but lost. The same thing happened in 1764 when a new Act was passed to strengthen the old one. "It was procured," wrote the Boston merchants, "by the interest of the West India planters, with no other view than to enrich themselves."

In 1763 at the end of the Seven Years War with England victorious in every instance against the French, the question arose of whether Canada or the captured sugar island of Guadeloupe and the slave trading port of Goree in the Senegal should be returned to the French. The West Indian Interest were bitterly opposed to the keeping of Guadeloupe, since its important sugar production would help glut the market and depress the price of sugar. The West Indians won the day and Guadeloupe went back to the French. Chatham was heavily criticised. "Some of his enemies objected to him that he did this out of partiality to his friend Beckford, and out of condescension to the particular interests of our Sugar Colonies; but in that I suppose they did him wrong," wrote Hardwicke, to the Duke of Newcastle.

Remembering how William Beckford was propelled by outraged pride at his rejection by the aristocracy makes his stance in the city more understandable. The ten years between 1760 and Beckford's death in 1770 was a period when the City discovered its political strength and a new sense of importance as a power base for Pitt, and also in its ability to break out vigorously on its own in a radical direction. Beckford was Pitt's most valued ally in the City and his ability to arouse the enthusiasm of the "middling" people, to fuse them into vigorous protest at the Government's handling of General Warrants in the famous Wilkes Affair and other attempts by the Court Party to extend royal prerogative, are part of constitutional history, rather than a book on the way the West Indians made their fortunes. Few men are able effectively to combine a political and a business career but Beckford managed it. He never received his political reward, it seems that he was genuinely fired by the causes he championed, and for this his contemporaries thought him naive and a demagogue. The City was in no doubt about him. As soon as he was dead, a statue of him was raised by public subscription, which stands today in the Guildhall, and it commemorates a typically impetuous and bellicose Beckfordian incident at Westminster in which he as Mayor and M.P. reduced young King George to silence by one of his ferocious frowns while he delivered the City's Grand Remonstrance on the restriction of freedom.

A more imaginative memorial has been unearthed in one of the "Episodes of Vathek" written by his son and heir, where he is portrayed as a Merchant Prince, sending out ships in every direction, trying to forestall Providence and control the future by his speculations; attentive to business, but indifferent to religion; anxious to have a male heir, importunate over women and other good things of life — "I shall certainly not wait a moment longer than I please."

The Alderman's son was indeed left England's Wealthiest Son, and the story of how he, a multi-millionaire, disposed of his fortune, is dealt with in a later chapter.

5

The Queen of Hell

The Jamaican-born Countess of Home wanted a full scale baroque organ in her new house in Portman Square. She discussed it with her architect, Robert Adam, and Adam drew detail drawings of what it would look like. The Countess was very fond of music and the organ was to be a major feature of her first-floor music room — a focus of attention and flattering conversation. But the Countess did not get her organ, though she got most of the other things she wanted. Perhaps she was dissuaded on the grounds of good taste — unlikely, since she was rich and stubborn enough to ignore such a consideration if it were the only objection; or was it the possible suffering of her neighbours — the house was part of an integrated frontage — also unlikely, such a thought would never occur to this egoistic lady. Much more probable was that a suitably grand instrument was not immediately available and the Countess would not wait to move into her new domain, but she loved music dearly; all sorts of music, and she made up for her disappointment by hiring her own Italian director of music and commanding lavish musical entertainments.

This poor fellows' life was never a smooth one. The well-rehearsed musical soirées had to allow for the mistress's caprice. Handel and jugglers, Thomas Arne and buskers off the street, a medley of improbable juxtapositions. One anecdote survives of such an evening. On a morning's outing, the Countess saw two negroes in self-created livery busking in the street with French Horns. Discovering that they too were from Jamaica, she cammanded them to come and amuse her guests that same evening. The musical majordomo was horrified at having to interpose jolly street players into his elegant chamber concert and hatched his plans accordingly. When the buskers arrived, they were taken down to the servants' quarters and liberally plied with the best Jamaican rum. When the time came for their musical debut before the elegant assembled guests they were both gloriously drunk and fast asleep. The Countess was apparently not amused.

Home House remains today a house of character and taste; its first owner, Elizabeth Countess of Home is much more difficult to pin-point. Her title came from her second husband William, the eighth Earl of Home, a Scottish peer and sometime military gentleman. She was born Elizabeth Gibbons in 1704 in Jamaica on the plantation of her prosperous father William Gibbons. She had a "creole" education, in other words she stayed at home where she may have had some private tuition for reading and writing, and spent the rest of the time with the household slaves. At sixteen she was married to James Lawes, eldest son of Nicholas Lawes, another of the Jamaican planter elite and an ex-Governor.

Elizabeth's new father-in-law was a much married and energetic figure who had come to Jamaica in 1663 and built up a substantial fortune. He has the credit of introducing the cultivation of coffee into Jamaica and of setting up its first printing press. His stamina for marriage was considerable — five wives, all of them widows. He was fond of saying that the female art of growing rich here in a short time was summed up in two significant words, Marry and Bury! But he himself outsmarted all his own, and collected their fortunes instead. His fourth wife bore him two sons, James and Temple, and the fifth, a daughter Judith Maria, who married Simon Luttrell, later to become the Earl of Carhampton. Their daughter Anne Horton was later to marry Henry, Duke of Cumberland, provoking a royal scandal and almost a constitutional crisis; their son Henry Lawes Luttrell, a man labelled by his contemporaries as a drunk, a liar and a brutal profligate, was the unhappy epicentre of a piece of particularly wicked electioneering malpractice at Middlesex in 1769 against the candidacy of John Wilkes.

James Lawes, the son and heir, having married in the family interest, for let us not forget that marriage in the 18th century was almost invariably a financial contract, decided he had no wish to remain in Jamaica, but to start a new life in England. So he took ship in 1732, but died within a year. Elizabeth was a childless, but doubly rich young widow of 29 in England.

Elizabeth was not immediately "greedily snapped up" by either a distressed bachelor or a rapacious widower, at least not for nine years. Considering her obvious wealth, she must have had a more than fair share of undesirable characteristics or habits to remain on the shelf so long. What passed for good manners in Jamaica was the subject of much ridicule and malevolent comment in England. Creoles were despised. Edward Long, member of a planter family and writer of a *History of Jamaica* published in the third quarter of the century was highly critical of Creole women. One of their problems, he wrote was their:

> constant intercourse from their birth with negro domestics, whose drawling, dissonant gibberish they insensibly adopt, and with it no small tincture of their awkward carriage and vulgar manners ... we may see ... a very fine young woman awkwardly dangling her arms with the air of a negro servant, lolling almost the whole day upon beds or settees, her head muffled up with two or three handkerchiefs ... When she roused from slumber, her speech is whining, languid and childish ... Her ideas are narrowed to the ordinary subjects that pass before her, the tittle-tattle of the parish, the tricks, superstitions, diversions and profligate discourses of black servants, equally illiterate and unpolished.

Another writer comments that Jamaican white women had "much of the quashee", scarcely more enlightened than their slaves, and Lady Nugent, that gossipy American wife of an English General, who kept a diary of her Jamaican posting wrote that "Mrs. C. is a perfect Creole, says little and drawls out that little, and has not an idea beyond her pen (plantation)".

Notwithstanding, in 1742 Elizabeth Lawes, widow, married William, Earl of Home. The Earl was an erstwhile military man who brought nothing into the marriage except his title and a reputation for gallantry under fire. His wife was fortyish — he cannot have hoped for an heir from that direction, and it must have been the money that attracted him. Within a year he deserted and we can only surmise at the possible reasons. In any case, he withdrew from the field without fortune, heir, and with little honour.

There are still Earls of Home today, though the line has been far from a direct one. The 14th Earl is better known to us as Alec Douglas-Home, who as Conservative politician in 1963 disclaimed his Earldom for life in order to sit in the House of Commons and head the Conservative Government of the day.

Little is known about the cast off Countess for twenty years until she re-surfaces in 1771 as lessee of one of the big new houses on the South side of Portman Square. From her windows she looked across virtually unbroken fields to the Hampstead Hills and decided she wanted her own house, to her own specification, on the yet unbuilt North side. So she called Robert Adam, the most fashionable and expensive of architects and commissioned him to build her just such a house as would allow her the fullest scope for her new ambition as a leading London hostess. She was now in her sixties.

New houses were rising in Marylebone "like exhalations" wrote one contemporary diarist. It was a time of ambitious and rapid building schemes. Military victories over Britain's mercantile competitors had brought economic prosperity. London was now the mercantile capital of the world, as well as the imperial seat of Government; the social centre for British society. People of wealth; people seeking privilege, power, or simply pleasure, flocked to it. Merchants in the City were restless to live in grander surroundings away from their counting houses and store rooms, but still within a carriage ride of their work. Housing, giving free play to rising social ambitions, became an urgent priority; a place to entertain, to make a show of servants, furnishings, deep carpets, table linen and good plate.

The demands of patrons, capricious, impatient but rich, the architects, addled with ale like Athenian Stuart, or crazed with commissions he daren't turn down, like James Wyatt, often incapable of supervising the progress of the work, dreaming up elegant, extravagant, challenging designs — all gave perfect excuses for endless delays and inflated bills. The builders were in their seventh heaven. The whole of Marylebone was one big building site and it was the chosen paradise of the great and the rich and the gullible. The sharpers, swindlers and social climbers moved in too. An extravagant Earl, a need for urgent credit, there were those who would oblige. Hogarth's "Marriage a la Mode" series tells the cautionary tale of one such bargain struck between the proud Earl who needs cash to complete his mansion and contracts to the marriage of his foppish son to the merchant's daughter — a contemporary common place which all Hogarth's viewers would recognise. Hogarth depicts this world of wealthy snobs with harsh insight, above all he documents the look and feel of his own con-temporary London as no other artist. Negro servants were one of the snobberies of the period — they appear in many Hogarth paintings. In his "Taste of High Life", a negro boy sits on the table elaborately dressed in livery and turban as a fine lady chucks him under the chin; in the fourth of "The Harlot's Progress" series, Mary, at the pinnacle of her profession, has a finely dressed negro boy to pour the tea. There is also an exquisitely dressed black boy in the Countess's Dressing Room in "Marriage a la Mode", while a fifteen or sixteen year old negro serves tea. There are similar figures in "Noon", in "The Industrious Prentice", in "Chairing the Member", and other social scenes by Hogarth. Black servants were indeed an emblem of rank or luxury, items of ostentatious display. Charles Duke of Richmond had Zoffany paint him out shooting in his grounds, accompanied by his elegantly dressed black slave boy. The black slave respectfully watching his master in the portrait of James Drummond, Fifth Earl of Perth, makes a point in even blunter terms — the slave boy wears a steel dog's collar. In fact, Matthew Dyer, a fashionable goldsmith advertised regularly that he made "silver padlocks for Blacks or dogs: collars etc", and that he would be pleased for a small extra charge to engrave the owner's Coat-of-Arms on them.

Black slaves had been filtering into England from the earliest days of the African trade. Ships' Captains brought them as part of their commission in kind, returning planters brought them for effect and show. They made good servants and more importantly, they did not have to be paid. As the flood of returning West Indians increased, so did the number of slave servants. They were publicly offered for sale in coffee houses or other places of public auction. The great Samuel Johnson bought Francis Barber, his black body servant, in 1752. Sir Joshua Reynolds kept one. John Baker, fashionable attorney and planter had Jack Beef who hunted with him. Admiral Lord Rodney was attended by his black slave servant on his deathbed. To have a team of black postillions or a parade of black liveried footmen was the height of chic.

Absentee planters and their families were arriving from the West Indies flushed with their importance as pillars of the Atlantic empire, and rich with the spoils of the sugar and slave trade. They formed closely connected networks by marriage and common trading interest and tended to settle in England in close community groups. They were more comfortable inside their own circle of friends whose education and background of interests were similar. A kind of social blackball tended to operate against the new arrivals; but it did not prevent them aspiring, and nothing could prevent them buying into exclusive residential conclaves.

In 1761 Henry William Portman inherited the Portman Estate which formed the West end of Marylebone and immediately gave instructions to his surveyors to prepare it for development. At more or less the same time, the end of hostilities with France, making sea voyages safer, marked the beginning of a new surge of West Indian families returning to Britain to look for roots. The development of the Portman Square area and the needs of rich West Indians coincided. The growth of Marylebone was spurred by the availability of West Indian money.

Marylebone today is an inner area of London densely covered with shops, office blocks and flats. It is difficult to imagine it as it was in the mid 18th century, essentially a country village, separated from the new palatial development around Cavendish Square, and sur-rounded by fields and country roads along which journeyed at one's peril in constant fear of attack from highwaymen and footpads.

From Oxford Street, which was the start of the Turnpike Road to Bath and the West country, North over Primrose Hill to Hampstead, was open country with scattered farms and fields of wheat — towards the west a small village around Paddington Green, and the manor house of Lileston with its dependent dwellings, and then open fields all the way to Kilburn Abbey. To the East, the Cavendish Estate development — a group of large Palladian mansions joined to Oxford Street in the South and with the beginnings of access roads from the square to the West and North, ending in fields or swamps, This was the new frontier of London, spreading steadily West, since the years of the Plague and the Great Fire.

Fear of plague and fear of fire, as much as anything, propelled the wealthier of citizens of London to seek new homes beyond the City walls. Daniel Defoe's horrifying and vivid eye-witness account of the Plague was published in 1722 and was widely praised and discussed, reminding all who read it — and this would mainly be the wealthier and thus more literate classes of the community — that the old City centre was a potential danger. To reinforce the message, a new plague was spreading from Turkey across Europe and the Merchant class of London were terrified for the possible interruption of trade. The real power of "A Journal of the Plague Year" was in no way diminished but rather enhanced by the knowledge that Defoe was only six when the Plague reached London and that his Journal was in reality only a work of fiction. The Great Fire was a dimmer memory. The City had been rebuilt in haste in brick this time, not wood, but on the same old street patterns. The big opportunity of a Grand City Design was lost in the scramble to keep the City's businesses open and save them from the competition of the growing and influential outports of the Western coast — Bristol, Liverpool and Southampton.

The first great London squares had been built before the Fire. Covent Garden was conceived for the Earl of Bedford by Inigo Jones in the first half of the 17th century as a "regular square surrounded by uniform houses in the classical tradition. The Earl got himself a stylish town mansion in clean air close to the City and the Court. He was also able to use his estate profitably by letting houses to affluent colleagues. And when the Covent Garden Piazza became fashionable, other landowners followed suit. Leicester Square was laid out in front of Leicester House (later to become identified with the Prince of Wales and his political supporters), and following the Plague (1665), St. James Square, Soho Square and Grosvenor Square were also laid out.

But none of the estate developments of the latter 17th century were co-ordinated or planned in any kind of way. Each square was a piecemeal scheme — hived off by the landlord to builders who in return for a cheap lease invested their capital — mostly labour — in running up skeleton houses as a speculation. Speculative builders then were no better than they are today and there were far fewer building regulations to protect the prospective householder. The standards were often poor and sometimes scandalous.

It was not until the mid-seventeen hundreds that this situation changed and the City fathers and other powerful parties began to demonstrate a greater sense of responsibility in planning and building, which inaugurates what came to be called the age of improvement. The story of this phase of Georgian history is superbly told by Sir John Summerson in *Georgian London*.

Politically too, it was not until the mid 18th century that big investors — the great estate holders and City institutions felt safe enough to launch major building. The uprooting of the Stuarts was followed by a succession of great and minor wars. People were not totally convinced that the Hanoverian Georges were in England to stay, until the last threat of the Jacobite pretension was removed. Then development began again and the London Square became the essential focus point to attract wealthy buyers. Henry Portman profited from the Cavendish experience. Not for him the mansions of the great landed Lords, nor the grand architectural effects, but an area of normal and spacious houses, securely tied in to neighbouring street layouts by its own main streets. In the North the New Road, later to become the Marylebone Road, had been cut in 1756 to enable the massive herds of cattle and droves of sheep and pigs necessary for supplying the metropolis to get to Smithfield without trampling through the new and elegant areas of the West End. For a while, the new road was the new frontier as Baker Street, Harley Street, Gloucester Place pushed up to it. The spirit of improvement was strong. In 1770 the Parish Act gave the St. Marylebone commissioners the responsibility for street lighting, cleaning and paving, in return for a householder's rate. Oxford Street and the more exclusive residential areas were soon paved.

Nevertheless up Oxford Street from Newgate Prison came the ragged and drunken processions surrounding the victims due for execution on public "hanging days" at Tyburn — now Marble

Arch. The gibbet, with its macabre burden was part of the London scenery until 1783 when the "quality" of Portman Square and other new squares complained of the danger to property caused by the rioting spectators. Dr. Johnson was sorry, "the public was gratified by a procession; the criminal supported by it", he said.

In 1774 the great Buildings Act aimed at making the outside of ordinary London houses as fire-proof as possible, by legislating away all wooden ornament and fancy window joinery. It also dealt with the slipshod methods of party-wall construction and to do this it was forced to lay down a structural code for different grades and sizes of speculative building. In one sense it led to the design of the whole street of standard houses, both neat and dignified, while Georgian standards were followed, but later to the dull Victorian suburban terrace street pattern.

No. 20 Portman Square, the new home built for the Countess of Home by Robert Adam, was one of the first important London houses to be constructed according to the new rules. Those fashionable Londoners who were ready to scoff at yet another hideous example of West Indian nouveau riche ostentation and bad taste were astonished when the house was eventually ready for its first party in 1776. The house was a masterpiece. Firstly the size of the house imposed; five large window bays instead of the usual three, allowing space for more rooms in which to entertain than was normal. The house faced into Portman Square so that main reception rooms were sunny and had a view over the Square which had recently been grassed and fenced for the exclusive use of the householders around the Square. The exterior was plain with discreet decoration in conformity with the new Building Act; London brick with Coade stone decorated panels. A pedimented Doric porch led into a hallway with fine mahogany doors, probably from her own West Indian estates, leading into the dining room and back parlour, beyond which lay a pleasant square garden and the stables. The staircase to the main reception rooms on the first floor was one of Robert Adam's most exquisite designs. The stairwell went straight up through the house to an elegant circular skylight which made the most of any available daylight. A single straight staircase led up to a half-landing and then divided into two branches which swept round the stairwell to the first floor landing. A delicate iron balustrade topped a fine mahogany handrail and the wall decoration was simple with small paintings by Zucchi. The most beautiful room was the music room on the first floor, with its finely modelled and painted ceiling, delicate stucco wall decorations and Angelica Kauffmann paintings; white marble fireplaces setting off the slim chairs and tables of the renowned craftsmen of the period like Chippendale and possibly some pieces designed by Adam himself. Over-looking the garden at the back was the small Etruscan room, designed to be the Countess's bedroom, using Robert Adam's own selection of Etruscan colours, black, cream and Pompeian red, a graceful tribute to Pompeian art made fashionable by recent diggings and discoveries in the old city. Her personal maid's room was linked to it from the floor above by its own spiral staircase. Another finely pannelled and furnished drawing room, sometimes known as The Ballroom completed the first floor .

All agreed as they paraded up and down the stairs and from room to room that the arrangement was superb: giving pleasure to the eye at each turning and vista; flattering the guests by "the luxury and good taste of the appointments"; a setting suitable for the mixing and meeting of the highest social class — perhaps even royalty itself. Indeed it is suggested that the Countess may in her old age have been grasping at a unique chance of social climbing — an opportunity of ingratiating herself and her social circle with the Duke of Cumberland, one of the King's brothers who had married secretly and against the Court interest, a commoner and a widow named Anne Horton. George III refused to receive them or recognise the marriage and let it be known that anyone who did receive the Duke or socialised with him and his new wife would not be received in Court.

Cumberland's attempts to re-establish himself, to increase his allowance from the Civil List and to get recognition for his children went on until his death in 1790, but in the meantime he needed opportunities of meeting, on neutral ground, politicians and other men of influence. His wife Anne Horton, was the daughter of Simon Luttrell whose wife was a daughter of Nicolas Lawes, the father of the Countess of Home's first husband. In the closely knit world of West Indian planters, Anne would be within the Countess's social circle and the idea of providing an elegant front for the Duke's incognito meetings may have flattered her. And it does help to explain why, at the age of 70, the Countess of Home built so lavish a house and set out to entertain on such a scale.

Some of the costs are known. The Countess opened a special account at Hoares Bank in November 1775 for the building costs. It shows payments totalling £3,500 to Robert Adam; £603 10. 0 to Joseph Rose, the famous stuccoist who also did Harewood House for Edwin Lascelles, £100 to Thomas Phillipson, carver and gilder, and £400 to Nebons, carvers, gilders and upholsterers. Multiply by fifteen and you will have a very rough equivalent in modern currency.

Most of what we know about the Countess of Home comes from the last years of her life when she was striving to become London's most audacious hostess. Linked to many of the most influential Jamaican families, she certainly became the magnet to which absentee West Indians, either visiting or intending to live in the metropolis were attracted. She was able to discuss property and recommend builders, and since the area in the immediate vicinity of Portman Square was in active development, it is not surprising that many West Indian families chose to make their homes here. Dozens of monuments and plaques in the various Marylebone churches testify to the fact that from 1770 many of the new houses were being taken by returning planters or by those whose fortunes were linked to them. To mention but a few, Florentius Vassall, one of Jamaica's largest plantation owners lived in Wimpole Street in the 1770's with his family, and one of the most famous and beautiful London hostesses of all time, Lady Holland, in whose salon the great statesmen and artists of Europe mingled, was also a Vassall. They were related to the Beckford family, two branches of which had houses on the South side of Portman Square opposite the Home House. The Erle Drax family of Barbados also had a house on the Square itself. Mrs Edwin Lascelles died at No. 16 Portman Square. One of the Lascelles of Barbados had a house in Wimpole Street as did the famous Mr. Barrett, immortalised by Charles Laughton a quarter of a century later — the Barretts had extensive plantations in Jamaica. Several Antiguan planters were here; Clement Kirwan and family in Upper Wimpole Street, and Nicholas Tuite, a planter who turned merchant and whose son became a prominent London banker, lived in St. Anne Street. General Haynes of Barbados had a house in Baker Street close to the corner of Portman Square, and Francis Ford, a rich Barbadian, died at his house in Portman Street in 1772. The Lawrences of Jamaica settled in Montagu Square — a huge clan, one of the best known of whom was Sir Thomas, the painter.

Marylebone grew quickly from the late 1760's. Not only West Indians absenting themselves from their plantations in the sugar boom which came with the Seven Years War, but all those with legitimate and illegitimate prizes and acquisitions from India and America flowed back to England to enjoy their new prosperity and consolidate their social standing. For all of these, Home House was a lodestar, the tangible example of one of theirs who had succeeded.

Elizabeth, Countess of Home, lived until 1784. Ironically in her final years, when all fleshly vanities should have mellowed, she was teased unmercifully by her nearest and most implacable neighbour, Mrs. Elizabeth Montagu. This lady, whose life-long ambition was to be London's leading hostess and whose intellectual salon in Hill Street got her the nickname of the "Queen of the Blue Stockings", decided that she too had to have a house in Portman Square, and an even grander house than her rival. "A small house, tight stays and strait shoes are plagues worthy to be put in the Litany of Worldy Things", she wrote. She bought the empty site on the North-West corner of the Square where the Portman Hotel now stands, and commissioned Athenian Stuart to build her a house "convenient for dwelling . . . cheerful as a place of retirement, ample for the devoirs of society and . . . calculated for Assemblies that it will suit all one's humours". Mrs. Montagu was fond of entertaining on a grand scale and through her Hill Street salons she had acquired a very wide range of acquaintances.

When she moved into her grand new house in 1781, the competition between the two elderly ladies whose front doors were scarcely a stone's throw apart grew, to the amusement of society. The young William Beckford living across the Square wrote a friend about an invitation to a Mrs. Montagu party:

> But what is this honour compared with that I accepted yesterday from another neighbour, a much more extraordinary lady than Madame Montagu, no less a person in short than the Countess of Home, known among all the Irish chairmen and riff-raff of the metropolis by the name, style and title of Queen of Hell. As her infernal majesty happens to have immense possessions not only, as of course, in the realms below, but on the island of Jamaica, which some think next door to them, she took it into her extremely eccentric head that, as a West Indian potentate, I ought to receive distinguished homage . . .

The Countess Elizabeth had some excuse for her upbringing. Social success in Jamaican society depended on ostentation. Richard Madden, writing in the first years of the next century of his personal experience in Jamaica says:

> The demon of colonial society is the spirit of rivalry in luxurious entertainments and apparel. If Mrs. S gives a party, it is incumbent upon Mrs. W to give a larger: if Miss A should happen to exhibit a tiara of pearls at the King's house, Mrs. B would go into hysterics if she could not display one of diamonds at the next ball . . . Grand entertainments abound . . . All the small sweet courtesies and tranquil enjoyments of friendly intercourse in minor circles . . . are unknown.

63

Mrs. Elizabeth Montagu with her "superior" upbringing had no such excuse.

So the "Queen of the Blues" faced the "Queen of Hell" and for three years the battle raged, until the Countess died, probably of sheer exhaustion. She was after all over eighty. In that year, the gardener who kept the centre of the Square on behalf of the Trustees made a list of the inhabitants. This is it:

*William Beckford	*Erle Drax
The Earl of Middleton	Lady Egmont
The Earl of Tankerville	*Sir Peter Parker
*Lady Home	*Admiral Lord Rodney
*Lord Maynard	The Earl of Ducie
Lady Tollemache	Samuel Whitbread
*Mrs. Beckford (senior)	

All those with stars* possessed plantations in the West Indies from which as absentee owners they derived their income. The hub of Marylebone was indeed a West Indian conclave.

When the Countess died she left her estate to her nearest surviving relation, William Gale, a minor at Westminster School, and when he died childless in 1794, a godson inherited and split up the property to sell it off. The bulk of Nicholas Lawes' very large residual estate, on which she had the life interest, reverted to the Earl of Carhampton and his family.

Home House has endured. It has had many owners, including the Rothchilds and it is now the Courtauld Institute of Art. It is the only Georgian house of any quality to survive the irresponsible developments of the 20th century and the bombs of World War II. It is all that remains of the large plantations of the Gibbons and the labour and lives of hundreds of slaves.

6

Our Beneficial System

I once stood coatless on a freezing winter's day in the gas chambers at Buchenwald and looked up at the ceiling and walls scratched by the frantic dying Jews — the naked evil of human aggression needed no further explanation.

Later, I visited the island of Goree, once a West African slave port. On its shore, stood the slaves' prison, a crouching grey stone blockhouse beside a pale blue lapping sea. Goree, Elmina, Bonny and Old Calabar, musical names refusing to admit their historical shame. A Griot might break the heart better, a poetic cry, rather than a document. Listen.

A hundred million of the damned — so moan the troubadours of Nakem when the evening vomits forth its starry diamonds — were carried away. Bound in bundles of six, shorn of all human dignity, they were flung into the Christian incognito of ships' holds, where no light could reach them. And there was not a single trader of souls who dared, on pain of losing his own, to show his head at the hatches. A single hour in that pestilential hole, in that orgy of fever, starvation, vermin, beri-beri, scurvy, suffocation, and misery, would have left no man unscathed. Thirty per cent died en route. And, since charity is a fine thing and hardly human, those amiable slavers were obliged when their cargo was unloaded to pay a fine for every dead slave; slaves who were as sick as a goat in labour were thrown to the sharks. Newborn babies incurred the same fate: they were thrown overboard as surplus . . . Half naked and utterly bewildered, the nigger trash, young as the new moon, were crowded into open pens and auctioned off. There they lay beneath the eyes of the all-powerful (and just) God, a human tide, a black mass of putrid flesh, a spectacle of ebbing life and nameless suffering.

The heap of slaves writhed, cries and moans were heard, bodies were trampled when the trader cracked his whip to wake up the niggers in the front rows. Those who had come to see the sight kept a respectful distance

65

and watched the priests who were here to proclaim the word of Christ, but could only fight down their disgust, hang their heads, and let their rosaries slip through their fingers . . .

(Bound to Violence. Yambo Ouologuem)

Goree. The name also of the swanky Georgian colonnade or piazza built along the quaysides of Liverpool's new dock for its booming West Indies and African Trade. The business community was delirious with the profits that were pouring in. Under the arches of Goree, the merchants could supervise the departure of their ships and give last minute instructions to their captains. "Watch that Fulani fellow at St. Louis, he'll sell you grave fodder if he can get away with it." "Mind you get a good price for the new cottons. We've got the colours they asked for." "If you accept Bills for your cargo in the Indies, make sure they're on a reliable House. I've given you a list of the ones we will accept." "Keep an eye out for those damn'd Frenchies." The captains who had a share in the profits and perhaps even owned a share of the ship, took good note. Liverpudlians were proud of their success in the African trade — proud that Liverpool was the second greatest port in the Kingdom because of it.

It had all begun so quickly. For most the 17th century there was scarcely a harbour — a kind of pool which was an inlet of the river Mersey. The river, though wide, was shallow and treacherous. Wind and tide, so important in the days of sailing, often viciously opposed. It was an uneasy perch for seagulls and the seagulls of the shipping trade were the nifty single-mastered coasters. Liverpool did well in the coasting trade and with the Irish trade too, which was almost coasting by the time a ship was off the westerly tip of Anglesey.

The town itself was scarcely more than a village clustered around the Pool — the Liver-Pool of course. Nevertheless, it was a proud and independent sort of place, whose freemen sponsored at least one M.P. in Parliament and vigorously opposed ship money. The great local family of the period were the Moores, who combined the roles of local landowners, and merchants, and often sat in the House of Commons for the town. In the Civil War it remained a Puritan stronghold in a predominantly Royalist area and its defence was organised by Edward Moore. Prince Rupert gazed impatiently down at it and muttered that it was "a mere crow's nest which a parcel of boys might take", but he was called away before the taunt could be put to the test, and as everyone knows, the Royalists lost the war.

Ironically, it was another war and a great epidemic which gave

Liverpool its first real taste of prosperity and its entry into the West Indian trade. The Dutch Wars which followed from Cromwell's aggressive attempt to seize the leadership of Europe's shipping trade from Holland, made the English Channel and Western Approaches a dangerous zone for merchant vessels — piracy could also be the sport of Kings. All shipping in and out of London had therefore to be convoyed or risk running the gauntlet. For many, the risk was too great.

Several important traders foresook London and came to Liverpool. There at least, ships crossing the Atlantic could pass directly round the North of Ireland and avoid the privateers. The second boost was fear of the Plague. Plague had frequently visited and ravaged the Southern counties within living memory. There was no reason to think that the Great Plague of 1665 would be the last, though it was the worst. Plague was bad for trade, so Mr. Smith, a great sugar baker from London, arrived in Liverpool and set up shop. It was the start of Liverpool's sugar refining industry, which is still active today.

The commercial expansion of the port and its immediate surroundings was quite apparent to the visitor in the 1670's. Blome, diarist and traveller, wrote that he found "divers eminent merchants, whose trade and traffic, especially with the West Indies, made it famous," and remarked that the neighbourhood "afforded in greater plenty and at reasonabler rates than most places in England such exported commodities as are proper for the West Indies." Liverpool was becoming a big international port. Property values rose. New warehouses and sugar refineries were built. A new class of thick-skinned and very wealthy merchants, such as the Clevelands and the Claytons, emerged. There was no grace or elegance about them, they preferred, it seems, to live on top of their money, in rooms over counting houses, stores or shops. They were the sort of men who were glad, for an agreed fee of £1,000 to ship 130 Jacobite rebels, whose death penalty had been transmuted to transportation and servitude in the colonies. They were shipped in irons, tight-packed, just like slaves and, having suffered the horrors of the middle passage, those which survived were auctioned in Barbados — the profits of which sale, plus any cargo brought back on the return journey, went into the merchants' pockets. Liverpool was a distinctly predatory place. Indeed, an Englishman did not have to have committed a serious crime in order to risk transportation. Kidnapping was a common activity in the English ports. It was also common for judges and magistrates to be associated with a colonial trade, or even a plantation. It was extraordinarily easy for these cynical men to turn a judgement into a profit. So short of labour were the West Indies at all times that they were prepared to take virtually anybody.

"No gaolbird can be incorrigible, but there is hope of his conformity here, as well as his preferment, which some have happily experimented", wrote Planter Jeffreson from St. Kitts. The transport of felons became a veritable minor industry, peopled by all of Hogarth's most revolting harpies, his courtly creeps, crooked judges and lawyers, leering jailers, drunken turn-keys, old viragos, venal ships' captains. At Bristol, Judge Jeffreys, who had himself done his bit for the "transportation" industry in sentencing traitors after the Monmouth Rebellion, called the Mayor before him on a charge of kidnapping felons to ship to the Caribbean. To "barbadoes" a person became a common verb for kidnapping.

For a long time, Liverpool merchants were more concerned with exploiting their direct trading links with the colonies. The colonies wanted woollen cloth for blankets and clothes, iron and pottery ware, coal and, increasingly, Manchester cottons, which were cheaper than the French or German cottons sold by London and Bristol merchants. All of these were available in districts neighbouring Liverpool; there was no need for her to become a manufacturing town herself. In return, her ships brought sugar, molasses for distillation into rum, tobacco, cotton and indigo. In sugar refining she overtook all other centres. She developed her coasting trade with her neighbouring ports of Chester, Whitehaven, Lancaster, Glasgow and they in turn supported and were supported by her. She fostered trade with Ireland and became the busiest port for two-way trade with that country. Liverpool became the driving force for a rapidly expanding industrial region. Her merchants called the tune and often provided the capital for manufacturers to expand. The merchant and the shipowner, not the manufacturer, went out and looked for markets and the manufacturer organized himself to meet the orders.

Liverpudlians came late to the slave trade, not out of any scruple but because they were too busy and because the profits did not look tempting enough. Slaves had been procured in Africa by the Portuguese since 1450 and sold in the Americas. The growth of British and French colonies in the seventeenth century called for a huge labour force which neither the numbers of free emigrants nor transported felons and rebels were able to satisfy. Earlier Portuguese and Spanish experience with black slaves was seized upon. Negro slaves were capable of being organised; they worked hard and they endured better than other races. Slave trading became a very lucrative trade in its own right. The British government, which regarded its own colonies as exclusive market gardens designed to benefit the mother-country, tried from the 1660's to create a monopoly of supply through its own chartered trading company owning forts and trading centres strategically placed along the slave coasts. This monopoly was resented both by the planters who believed they were overcharged and demanded free trade, as well as by the shippers and merchants in England who wanted a slice of a profitable business. Bristol, Liverpool, Glasgow, Lancaster, Exeter and Chester attacked the monopoly with every weapon they could find, and in 1698 it was broken. The merchants of Bristol quickly entered the trade, and by 1700 had 46 ships in the trade. "The Labour of Negroes is the Principal Foundation of our Riches from the Plantations," crowed William Wood in 1718 in a national trading survey, "The African trade ... is the Spring and Parent whence the others flow."

Estimates of the total numbers of Africans transported during the years of slavery have varied from 10 million to over 100 million, but the most reliable figure appears to be that of 15 million. Of that 900,000 were taken in the 16th century, 2,750,000 in the 17th century. The figure rose in the eighteenth — the century when sugar was king — to 7 million and falls as abolition bites, to 4 million in the 19th century.

Liverpool's entry into the slave trade was uncharacteristically modest — just one vessel of 30 tons in 1709 and then trade did not get under way effectively till 1731 when the Spanish colonial market for slaves suddenly opened up. Then Liverpool's merchants, hitherto profitably occupied in other kinds of colonial trade, felt that this was their moment. The number of ships sailing to Africa dramatically increases. In 1731 fifteen; in 1737 thirty-two; in 1752 fifty-eight putting Liverpool substantially ahead of London and Bristol to become the principal slaving port in Europe, a position it held for the rest of the century. Such an advance could not be made without profound changes to the port itself. New building went on continuously. The Port of London, hampered by ancient privileges and rights, by stubborn wharfingers, lightermen and not least by the cobweb-covered administrators of the city, remained changeless. But Liverpool, more single-minded, its corporation closely involved in the business of the city, all of which in some way depended on the rapid movement of ships in and out, decided on a bold policy of

investment. The Corporation itself financed an advanced programme of improvement and building. In 1715 the Old Dock
replaced the Pool and before the end of the century four more
docks were added.

The King's Dock handled most of the American trade. Here
were the bonded tobacco warehouses built and rented out to
H. M. Customs by the Corporation: the biggest corn warehouses
and a large number of naval suppliers, roperies, anchor smithies,
block makers, sailmakers. There was the Salthouse Dock which
handled the salt from the Cheshire mines, an increasingly valuable
export and frequently used as ballast for ships making for the
Guinea coast.

While the West Indies and the slave trade together were responsible for the spectacular fortunes being made in Liverpool, it
was fast becoming an international port in the widest context.
Ships sailed to and from the Baltic, to Spain, Portugal and the
Mediterranean ports and the whale fisheries in the South and
North Atlantics. To cater for this growing traffic the Queens Dock
was built, "the newest, largest and best furnished at an expense
of 25,000 pounds" according to the Liverpool Guide. Next to
the Salthouse Dock new ship-building yards had sprung up. The
Old Dock, previously mentioned, handled most of the West India
and African trade, surrounded by the warehouses of the merchants
who specialized in this trade. This dock also focussed much of
the coastal trade — a great many small vessels, bringing corn
from agricultural areas and taking back West Indian produce.
Traditionally these coastal traders were the main means of dif-
fusing goods to and from the surrounding areas. A start was made
to deepen channels and widen rivers towards Manchester in the
mid-century. James Brindley began with the widening of the
Sankey Brook from St. Helens to the Mersey and, in 1758, the
Duke of Bridgewater began a new canal to bring coal from his
inland mines to the port, together with a new private dock to
handle all the barges and lighters which carried the inland trade.
From these beginnings a network of new canals developed rapidly,
linking Liverpool with the main centres of Midland and North
Country trade. Liverpool merchants put up much of the money
for them. The cost of carrying goods from Liverpool to Manchester
by horseback had been 40 shillings a ton. With the new canals
it fell to 6 shillings a ton. The impetus given to trade of bulk
goods such as coal, iron and salt was immediately felt.

While money was being spent on the tackle of commerce,
whether in hard stone quays, brick warehouses or scraping the
river bed, little or nothing was done for the citizenry. Liverpool

as a place was becoming richer, and investing heavily in its business structures so as to become even richer, but the majority of its people lived in poverty and squalor. The large population of seamen, mainly the dregs of society, the availability of cheap rum — not surprising a visitor in 1795 declared, that every seventh house was open for the sale of liquor. James Stonehouse, the son of the owner of the slave ship Mary Ellen remembered the atmosphere of his early life:

> Scarcely a town by the margin of the ocean could be more salty in its people than the men of Liverpool of the eighteenth century, so barbarous were they in their amusements, bull-baiting, cock and dog fightings and pugilistic encounters. What could we expect when we opened no book to the young and employed no means of imparting knowledge to the old, deriving our prosperity from two great sources, the slave trade and privateering, Swarming with sailormen, flushed with prize money, was it not likely that the inhabitants generally would take a tone from what they beheld and quietly countenanced,

Inland conditions in growing manufacturing areas were scarcely better. Primitive working conditions, brutal use of women and children were more the rule than the exception in the trades which were the foundations of the new industrial order.

To trade for slaves on the African coast, Liverpool merchants collected together a mixed cargo thought to be most suitable for bartering with the local dealers or chiefs with whom they would have to trade. From experience such a cargo would consist of cottons, iron bars, guns, pottery, rum or brandy, various kinds of trinkets — beads, mirrors, shells. The ship with its cargo sailed from England to the slave coast where it traded its goods profitably and bought slaves with other luxury goods such as gold dust and ivory if available. The ship then sailed with its human cargo to the Caribbean or up to the mainland American colonies, where the slaves, less the inevitable shipboard losses, were sold at a second profit. The ship then returned to its home port with colonial goods, with cash or bills of exchange, or all three, which provided a third profit. It was a neat commercial system, fitting perfectly the economic theories of the age and providing the maximum of gain for the venturers. It was known as the triangular trade because of its three legs, the most notorious being that from Africa to the Indies through the Middle Passage with a live cargo. The brutality of this trade has been graphically documented in dozens of books and even more recently in a TV series, and it is not the purpose of this book to cover such familiar territory yet again. What concerns us here is how involvement in such a trade turned Liverpool and many of its citizens into one of the most prosperous cities in the United Kingdom and so primed the pump of the new technologies, that the increasing revolutions of the flywheels in the mills of Yorkshire and Lancashire and in the foundries and potteries of Staffordshire, became imperceptibly a real Industrial Revolution.

Cargoes to trade for slaves were drawn from a wide variety of manufacturer. A typical list in its original form is the following, found in the papers of Captain Lutridge of Whitehaven, but equally applicable for any Liverpool sailing.

Scheme of a Cargoe to Purchase Slaves on the Gold Coast.

60	Bijnta pants @ 16/6
40	nigani pants @ 15/-
100	fine Brawles @ 5/-
50	Chints @ 7/6
40	fine small nucanes @ 8/9
30	fine blew Balfs 18 yds. each 21/-
30	Camdames @ 16/-
80	Cotton Romalls @ 9/6
30	Coppes @ 13/6
40	Pohotaies @ 9/-
30	Strip'd callanues @ 29/-
10	Fine Searsuckers @ 20/-
200	checked Chilais @ 20/-
800	lb. of Courries @ 85/-
30	Chints blew and white @ 20/-
4000	Azzangoes @ 60/- p.m. (i.e. 1000)
10	English Bourbaye Stuffs
360	lb. purple black white olwta bead @ 11d. lb
1000	blue and light green Perpets @ 10/6
70	Green long ells @ 29/-
20	Course blew sayes @ 31/-
1300	old sheets @ 17d
800	brass pans 9-cwts. 1-qr. 8-lbs. @ 140/-
60	Guinea Carpets @ 2/9
200	lb. Tobaccos @ 6d. per lb.
385	Barrs iron qr.8-lbs. @ 16/10/- per tun
3	doz. Coarse hatts @ 15d
40	pair blankets @ 3/6
400	Cags tallow 44-cwt.3. 12-lbs. @ £29 per tun
400	pewther Basons 3 lbs. each @ 8d. per lb.
30	—do— 4-lbs.
30	—do— 2-lbs. @ 8d. per lb.
30	—do— 1-lb.
20	screw Jugs @ 10/6

1227	gallons spirits in 6 guinea (bottles)
40	wecker Bot of 'Do'
30	Caggs 'Do'
400	trading arms @ 7/3
75	musquets @ 8/3
75	bucaneers @ 11/6
45	gun powder repackt into 30 half lb:222 qr @ 57/6
1	gross knives @ 29/-
36	gross pipes
20	casks spirits @ 10/-

Such transactions had already attained a degree of sophistication. Certain colours and qualities of cloth, English made guns in preference to Dutch, sharp pointed knives like a butchers. Alcohol or spirits as they were called, were essential to weaken the bargaining power of local trader or chief, and formed a major part of any cargo. Victuals were necessary, both for the crew and for the slaves who were to be transported.

Nor did it end there. The islands were themselves a continuing market for English goods. Clothes for slaves, food supplies, building materials, equipment for sugar production, farming implements, cannons and weapons for defence, furniture for planters and merchants' houses — the list was endless, the demand continuously growing.

The cost of entering the trade was not necessarily high, men and women too with small capital combined to share the cost of building and equipping a ship. This in fact was the normal pattern. It enabled men like William Aspinall and Thomas Leyland to get started. A sixteenth, or multiples of a sixteenth, was the usual division. A round trip would take over a year before the investors could add up their benefits or losses. There were losses — storm, capture by enemy ship or privateer were quite frequent, and excused the high profits of 100% or more from a successful voyage. It also explains why the sharing system came about. It was a form of insurance, spreading the risk. Not only merchants and their families were involved. Captains, quite apart from their normal commissions might have a share in the voyage and so might dozens of other tradesmen. The slave trade was no hole-in-the-corner affair, hundreds of humbler citizens were enriched by it. "Almost every order of people," says a Liverpool writer in 1795 "is interested in a Guinea cargo . . . He who cannot send a bale, will send a bandbox . . . It is well known that many of the small vessels that import about an hundred slaves are fitted out by attorneys, drapers, ropers, grocers, tallow-chandlers, barbers, tailors etc. of whom some have one eighth, some a fifteenth, some one-twenty-second share."

In 1701 the annual export of bulk goods to the Guinea Coast was only £83,280. By 1786 it was £583,052.

The voyage of the *Hawke* in 1779 is well-documented. She cost the owners £400 and £2,000 to equip and arm. She carried cargo to the value of £3,000. This cargo was traded for 368 slaves, and £2,700 worth of ivory. In the West Indies the slaves fetched almost £10,000 after expenses were deducted. Some extra freight worth some £800 was also collected. The profit for the voyage amounted to £7,000. She sailed a second time the following year, and this time she picked up in addition some £4,500 of cargo to bring back to Liverpool which was profitably sold for £7,500. En route she took a prize which fetched £3,700. A total profit of some £14,000

Absolute credence cannot be given to 18th century account books anymore than it can today. The value of cargoes outward bound were frequently exaggerated. Goods charged at first class quality were often seconds or even rejects. This is a common trading trick which modern manufacturers still attempt to pull on unsophisticated markets. Often the shipper was also the whole-saler, or even manufacturer of the goods and wrote out his prices at the top figure to favour himself against his partners or for insurance purposes. It is likely therefore that profits were in fact higher than stated.

To these gentlemen of fortune, slaves were simply items on an invoice, commodities like cattle, tricky to pack and carry to their destination in good condition. The instructions issued by experienced merchants to their captains read like a veterinary surgeon's textbook.

In the 1780's Liverpool alone was estimated to be making a clear profit of £300,000 from the slave trade. There was even a street called Negro Row where slaves were sometimes sold by auction in the shops, warehouses and coffee-houses. Iron hand-cuffs, leg shackles and thumb screws were displayed in the local ship chandlers' windows.

The questions which crowd in when contemplating this un-relieved saga of commercial successes, based so obviously on human suffering on a massive scale, are those of 20th century "civilised" man. How could they do it? Did it even bother them? Did it rub off on them?

We know little about these men beyond the commercial records, customs returns, details of cargoes and ship sailings to be pieced together from local records. They wrote no diaries, consigned no intimate thoughts to letters, attracted the attention of no Scouse Boswell. The attitudes of the vast majority as recorded in petitions, pamphlets and instructions to their M.P's are purely materialist, brooking no interference with their methods, their markets or their profits. The slave trade was the "beneficial system". No one felt in the least guilty about it. To talk of a tender conscience was sentimental folly. Conscience was something you developed when you were losing, or wanted to cover your tracks. Bristol, for instance, so long the most important slaving port, had lost all hope of catching Liverpool by the end of the 18th century. Suddenly it began taking a high moral tone, viz. The 1799 New Bristol Guide.

> The ardour for the trade to Africa for men and women, our fellow creatures and equals, is much abated among the humane and benevolent merchants of Bristol. In 1787 there were but 30 ships employed in this melancholy traffic; whilst the people of Liverpool in their indiscriminate rage for commerce and for getting money at all events have nearly engrossed this trade, incredibly exceeded London and Bristol in it, employ many thousands of tons of shipping for the purpose of buying and enslaving God's rational creatures, and are the vendors of the souls and bodies of men and women! to almost all the West Indian Islands!!!

Already by the 1750's there was hardly a corner of the United Kingdom which had no contact with the African and West Indian trade.

M. Postlethwayt, a prolific writer on the theory and practice of commerce in the Mercantilist period, wrote in his 1746 pamphlet, The National and Private Advantages of the African Trade, considered:

> . . . our West-Indian and African Trades are the most nationally beneficial of any we carry on . . . the extensive Employment of our Shipping in, to, and from America, the great brood of seamen consequent thereupon, and the daily Bread of the most considerable part of our British Manufacturers, are owing primarily to the Labour of Negroes; who, as they were the first happy Instruments of raising our Plantations; so their Labour only can support and preserve them, and render them still more and more profitable to their Mother-Kingdom. . .

In fact the triangular trade itself was only part of the total commerce which linked up with it. First there was the increase in shipbuilding — special ships had to be fitted up, adaptable to carry conventional cargoes on one voyage and convert to slaves on another. They had to be fast, in order to keep the slave-carrying leg of the trip as short as possible and also to avoid capture.

It is estimated that in 1795 there were up to 3,000 shipwrights working in Liverpool, and many of the bigger ones were themselves slave traders. Baker and Dawson was one of the bigger companies doing both. Dawson was a specialist. He negotiated with the Spanish in 1783 the contract to supply her colonies with slaves at the rate of at least 3,000 a year, and if possible shipping them to St. Domingo, Cuba, Savannah and Curacao. The contract was immensely lucrative and it enabled Dawson to finance the building of special ships of 300 tons and over — twice as big as most slavers — in order to double his turnover in half the time. When the contract was due for renewal, Dawson's agents in Spain were instructed to spare no expense to obtain the new seven year deal and they spent almost £2,000 in slush money, or the approximate cost of 200 slaves on the African coast, to get it.

The Cunliffes were an energetic merchant family. Foster Cunliffe, who was Mayor on several occasions in the first half of the 18th century, was deeply involved in the African trade. With his sons as partners, he equipped four specialised slaving ships to hold 120 slaves, each of whose captains were instructed to ply between Africa and the West Indies or the North American plantation colonies. Their venture was so successful that they were able to purchase West Indian rum, sugar and other specie for sale in England which filled 12 ships. Ellis Cunliffe represented Liverpool in the Commons from 1761, was "a sure friend" to the Duke of Newcastle, and had exclusive trading connections with America, being one of the first to import Maryland cotton. He was knighted in 1756 and made a Baronet in 1759. The family has continued to the present day. The 9th Baronet lives in modest comfort in Hertfordshire.

The hard facts of the business are astonishing enough. Between 1783 and 1793 ships from the Mersey shipped more than 300,000 slaves producing an income of £14½ million. In the ten years between 1795 and 1804, the Liverpool merchants shipped 323,770 slaves from Africa, against London's share of 46,405 and Bristol 10,718. The huge increase in shipping which this indicates is shown by the known statistics.

In 1751 Liverpool owned 220 ships totalling 19,174 tons worked by 3,319 men. In 1801 Liverpool owned 821 ships totalling 129,470 tons worked by 12,315 men. In 1751 the total tonnage of British and foreign ships entering or leaving Liverpool was 65,406 tons; in 1791 it was 539,676 tons, and by 1835 it was 1,768,426 tons.

Not every year, not every voyage brought an inevitable improvement in fortune to reward hard work and high risk. The 18th century was a period of intensive commercial rivalry, which could only be settled by war. Trade was interrupted at such times, then an army of sailors, shipwrights, chandlers, manufacturers of chains and implements, would all turn their minds to their favourite hobbies of privateering and smuggling. The privateers of Liverpool were as notorious or famous, as discussed and cheered, as the City's aggressive footballers today. Mettlesome and rapacious, their exploits fill several books. They returned to Liverpool with profitable prizes, they were even known to engage British warships in error. It was a violent kind of fun which the Liverpool privateers made particularly profitable.

Smuggling of brandy and spirits was the speciality of the Southern ports like Poole and Brixham and Plymouth; Liverpool's speciality was slaves, not into the United Kingdom of course, but into the Spanish and even the French colonies. The British fleet so dominated the African coast during the century that neither the French nor the Spanish could stock their plantations quickly enough. Official trade with the British or their colonies was strictly regulated, so an elaborate system of smuggling went on which made an interesting variation on the triangular trade. Bristol had the biggest share of this traffic in the early years of the century, but by the middle, Liverpool had completely dominated it. In 1757 for instance, there were 176 Liverpool ships involved, giving an annual profit of £250,000.

Though the risks were higher, the profits too were higher. After Abolition, smuggling became the only way the British could participate in the trade, not to British islands, but to the Spanish and Portuguese colonies such as Cuba and Puerto Rico whose sugar plantations were rapidly developing, and into Brazil and Central America as well.

William Aspinall was a sail-maker in 1761, who became a merchant and then an extremely active participant in the slave trade. Not only was he engaged in the direct trade on the Guinea Coast, but he had fingers in other profitable pies. The Jamaican slave mart was the biggest in the Indies. It handled incoming slaves, not only for the British colonies, but for the Spaniards as well, who not only offered a better price, but paid in cash as well, much to the anger and frustration of the British planter who could usually only offer produce or a bill. Aspinall and Hardy were a slave brokerage firm trading heavily in the 1790's.

Aspinall, Roscoe and Lace was a merchant house formed with its very successful slaving Captain, Ambrose Lace, who became a rich man on the proceeds and was able to come ashore in great comfort. But Aspinall's place in the history books is assured by his association with Captain Hugh Crow, that jovial and rascally slaving skipper who made the last legal slaving voyage in July 1807 in the *Kitty Amelia* owned by Aspinall, and who also wrote in his well-seasoned memoirs of the despair of his African friends at the news of Abolition, and their amazement that the English King should want to take away their livelihoods.

The Aspinall family were partners in the company which owned the *Zong*, a slaver involved in one of the most cynical and revolting acts against a slave cargo, which is on the record. In September 1781, Captain Luke Collingwood in the *Zong* sailed from St. Thomé, the Island off the present Nigerian coast with a cargo of 470 slaves and his own crew of 17. They were bound for Jamaica. Either through bad navigation, drunkeness or for sinister motives, the ship went down wind past Jamaica and had to work its way back. It had not been a good voyage before this happened; 60 slaves and 7 crew members died. Now many others were desperately ill. The Captain made his calculations and explained to his officers that if the slaves met a natural death, the loss would fall upon the owners of the ship, but if they were thrown overboard alive on a pretext of necessity for the ship's safety, the insuring underwriters would have to pay. The officers' profits were also at risk. It did not take much persuading to get them to weed out the sick and toss them over the side. Altogether they deliberately drowned 137 slaves. On Collingwood's return to Liverpool, the owners claimed the full insurance compensation. Despite the extraordinary nature of the evidence, the insurers lost, the jury decided that the case of slaves was the same as if horses had been thrown overboard.

The Abolitionists, whose campaign was making slow headway, took the *Zong* as a cause celebre, and Parliament passed an Act to protect the insurance companies from claims of throwing slaves overboard!

Captain Roberts was another notorious shipper. On the slaving coast he enjoyed stirring up chiefs and kings to savage sorties against their neighbours in order to fill his ships, or firing a cannon or two into a town with which he was trading to hurry things up. He had a great thirst for undiluted Jamaica rum, and earned the name of "Bully" for an incident in which he shot and pitched overboard a wayward matelot. In 1767 he sailed for the Caribbean with a cargo of 400 male slaves and 230 females. He struck bad weather and other delays. Slaves began to die — water had to be rationed, so Roberts threw the sickest overboard in order to save his supplies. He lost a hundred slaves before reaching Jamaica, but he sold the remaining 530 at an average of £60 a head and showed a huge profit.

As the slave trade snowballed and more and more ships had to be equipped, crewed and cargoed, it was impossible for Liverpool merchants to finance it all themselves. Many of the successful merchants indeed extended their trading interests into financing and banking. Arthur and Benjamin Heywood, owners of several African slavers, progressed from merchants to banking. The Heywood Bank was founded in 1773 and prospered throughout the 19th century. They also had a woollen manufacturing business in Wakefield. The Heywoods were prominent citizens in Liverpool and Manchester, and considered as gentlemen of the highest moral and social qualities. Benjamin gave up for ever the sordid cut and thrust of dockside trading for the world of high finance. He was a member of the Liverpool Fire Insurance Company and preferred the more congenial atmosphere of the exclusive Billiards Club in Manchester and a devotion to the philanthropic institutes of the working class. His generosity and zeal in this work, together with his "impeccable" business activities were marked with a Baronetcy in 1838. He had indeed made himself into a gentleman with unimpeachable credentials.

William Gregson, Francis Ingram, Robert Fairweather, Jonas Bold, Thomas Fletcher, and many others, owed their first steps into the respectable world of banking to the capital accumulated in successful slaving ventures. Moreover, though it was Liverpool merchants and seamen who were openly and eagerly engaged in the slave trade, the London commission agents, in the dual capacity of broker and banker, were providing cash and credit on a large scale.

They remained aloof and insulated in a world of beautifully engraved Bills of Exchange and other artefacts of high finance and avoided both the criticism of the Abolitionists and the aura of guilt association, which settled over the outports of Bristol and Liverpool.

Thomas Leyland was a gentleman of fortune in several ways. He originally migrated from Yorkshire to Liverpool as a clerk to a shipping company. He borrowed from friends and bought his way into a share of a cargo. In 1776 however, he won a lottery for £20,000, married his former employer's daughter, and went into the slave trade on a big scale. He became one of the wealthiest ship owners, and was also Mayor of Liverpool in the last quarter of the century. With the capital he made from the African trade he went into banking. In 1802 he was senior partner of the bank

of Charles and Roscoe, Leyland and Roscoe, while in 1807 he settled on a more durable banking partnership with another slave merchant called Bullins. He died a millionaire. The firm of Leyland and Bullins prospered throughout the 19th century and was eventually amalgamated in the North and South Wales Bank Limited.

Quite apart from the direct benefits of the trade, all kinds of other benefits sprang from each and every ship movement. There were warehouse rents, custom duties and other taxes, various commissions, bribes and other slush monies, banking and insurance commissions, docking dues, maintenance costs — all adding to the general well-being and prosperity of the port, providing hundreds of new jobs and boosting neighbouring towns and industries.

Liverpool's gentlemen of fortune are a veritable army of merchants and seamen, lawyers and bankers, builders and engineers, shopkeepers and ordinary citizens, who took with both hands in their sharp-clawed climb to wealth and gave little in return. They left it to the future generations to redeem the history of blood-stained wealth and human misery.

When abolition came, many notabilities and pillars of society were aghast at the impending loss and predicted bankruptcy and ruin on a vast scale. Failures there were, but Abolition came when other market opportunities were already manifest. Liverpool merchants like John Gladstone were looking East to India and West to the increasingly important American States, and Liverpool was ready and able, with its powerful trading companies and modern port facilities, to develop into an even more powerful international trading centre.

1. Alderman William Beckford: 'the stuff of headlines and lawsuits and general outrage'

Chapter 4   Page 43

2. The sugar plantation was, in effect, a factory in the fields

Johnny, Newcome landing in the W.ᵗ Indies.

Johnny situated as Clerk of Stores.

Johnny on a Country excursion.

Johnny enjoying the sports of the field.

Johnny enamoured with Nymphs bathing.

Johnny Preachee and Floggee poor Mungo.

3. A Gentleman of Fortune lampooned at a shilling a sheet
Chapter 9   Page 104

4. What passed for good manners in Jamaica was the subject of much ridicule in England

5. Black servants and slaves were an emblem of rank or luxury, items of ostentatious display in English society. They were publicly offered for sale in coffee houses or other places of public auction

Chapter 5 Page 57

6. *Left above* West Indian money fertilized one part of Britain that conventional methods of growth might never have reached

Chapter 8   Page 101

7. *Left below* Penrhyn Castle: 'this enduring and eccentric monument to an obsession'

Chapter 8   Page 97

8. *Below* 'The great hall of Penrhyn Castle is a tour de force, floored with polished slate from the Penrhyn quarries'

Chapter 8   Page 98

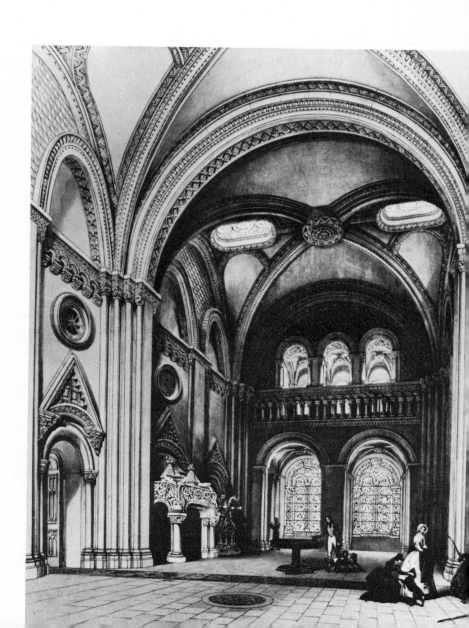

9. Xanadu on a Wiltshire hilltop, Fonthill Abbey. 'Mysterious hooded figures with large wax torches lit the way up to the grand staircase'

Chapter 10 Page 124

10. Under the arches of Goree, the Liverpool merchants could supervise the departure of their ships

Chapter 6   Page 66

11. London was deeply involved in the slave trade

Chapter 9   Page 105

7

The Sweet Ayre of England

Bath Abbey is one of the monastic churches that Henry VIII's secretary Cromwell "knocked about a bit", and sold off, stripped of its lead, furnishings, roof beams and anything else which could raise cash. The city of Bath inherited the Abbey as a ruin open to the sky, and it was eventually restored as a grand, but lugubrious gothic pile in the 17th century, to which later generations made well-meaning but dreary additions. If the Abbey ever had any architectural merit, it has not survived. It has, however, collected one other claim to our curiosity. As the fashionable parish church for the booming 18th century spa, the Abbey has become in the words of the historian J. C. Plumb "a vast lumber room of the wealthy dead". Here, moreover, there are more funerary monuments to West Indian planters and their families than in any other church in Britain. These people who migrated back across the Atlantic in the late 17th and more and more throughout the 18th, were to Bath like the swallows of spring; they arrived in season in a flock, certain in their numbers and family connections, never to be short of "acquaintance", or to risk being snubbed by the English gentry. They arrived on limping wings, exhausted and often dying. Their summer nest became their last resting place. Planters, merchants, lawyers, sea captains, widows, children. If we had no other evidence than church monuments, we could establish Bath for West Indians as an important attraction, a residential centre, a hope often misplaced.

Health, or rather the lack of it, was one of the main reasons for the return of so many Britons who went out as adventurers to make their fortunes. They ached above all "to sucke in some of the sweet ayre of England".

Throughout the 18th century, the arts of medicine remained in a grossly retarded state. No basic principles were agreed and doctors, with their own ideas, prescribed cures by the wildest guesswork. Hippocrates' ancient "humoral pathology", by which it was said all illnesses derived from the "humours of the body, whether sanguine, choleric, melancholic or phlegmatic" was still widely practiced as it was in Chaucer's day by the good doctor who:

> The cause of every malady you'd got,
> He knew, and whether dry, cold, moist or hot;
> He knew their seat, their humour and condition,
> He was a perfect practising physician.

Current fashionable theories of the 18th century were no more scientific, and when it came to cures, the methods favoured tended to be wholly similar — artificial raising of blisters, blood-letting, the panacea to cure all ills from headache to severe cancer, purging, the prescribing of toxic drugs and the inducement of vomiting.

Through this totally inadequate medical barrier, the great social killer diseases rampaged unchecked. Smallpox, measles, all the venereal diseases, cholera, diphtheria, typhoid fever.

If you survived at all it was seldom without permanent damage or weakness. But in addition to these, all Europeans going to the tropics found themselves exposed to a further battalion of diseases, yellow fever, malaria, all kinds of parasitical worms, amoebic dysentery — known as fluxes — the bites — poisonous or fatal of every kind of insect and reptile. Nor did anyone living or working in the tropics yet understand the preventive aspects of dress, diet or correct balance of body salts. The soldiers wore heavy woollen uniforms in the mid-day sun or in tropical rain storms. Manual workers were fed on gruel, planters stuffed and drank themselves silly.

Even today when killer diseases have been overcome, the European entering the tropics has to take careful health precautions in order to survive. I have often met my countrymen in remote tropical areas whose recurring nightmare is the fear of physical accident or illness in a country where no proper medical facilities exist nearby, and where cross-infection, even in the best hospitals, is the biggest killer. The early colonists and their families faced appalling risks in total ignorance. A military posting to the West Indies came to be regarded as a death sentence. Child-bearing was a major hazard; almost any complication was terminal. The European took with him his European diseases, influenza, syphilis, measles, to which he had a degree of toleration, but which ran like wildfire through the local tribes or the slave gangs.

Without recourse to effective drugs or medicines, no-one anywhere was ever quite free of actual pain, or the threat of it. Quite minor ailments like toothache, skin cancers, minor cuts, chronic headaches, became debilitating illnesses. Any deap-seated constitutional weakness like gout, cancer, rheumatic fever, heart-trouble, must have been agony, continual and inescapable. In the midst of ignorance and suffering, any possible remedy was attempted. For the poor there were potions and pills handed out by travelling pedlars and newsmen. For the moneyed the great popular "cure-all", of the 18th century, was the hot mineral water springs of the Spa towns in Britain and on the Continent. Even the medical profession, whatever their pet theories, agreed together that Spa water, if not actually miraculous, was certainly a God-given instrument of healing.

The popularity of Bath owes itself partly to this wide-spread desire for relief from pain and the hope of a return to healthy life; but partly also to the shrewd and courageous exploitation of this marketable resource by local businessmen and landowners. Anyone who could afford it wanted to go there.

The selling of Bath, or to be more precise, the selling of Bath as a desirable watering place, is one of the great advertising and marketing stories of the period. On the one hand, that extraordinary character Beau Nash imposed himself as the Spa's Master of Ceremonies to such effect that the rough customs and manners of visitors in public places were quite transformed. His rigid code of conduct, suppressing duelling, regulating gaming, establishing rules for betting, requiring the correct attire at balls and assemblies and for dealing with many of the human sharks who fed off gullible invalids, did a great deal to establish Bath as a Spa for fashionable society. Further, he saw that invalids and relatives accompanying them needed a programme of entertainment that relieved them of the need to invent one themselves and so he organised concerts, theatre, assemblies and balls, conducted with decorum and ceremony. He firmly established the habit of promenading, spaced out by a bathing regime, public breakfasts, coffee and tea sessions, shopping and talk.

Bath, at the start of the 18th century, was already a popular resort, but singularly lacking in comfort and amenities. The Baths themselves were open-air affairs, over-crowded, filthy, gross, and sometimes more like an open sewer. The lodging houses and inns were also over-crowded and dirty. The parish church was the only public amenity, yet members of the Royal family in search of health, or fertility, or both, visited; the Courtiers followed, and the fame of Bath was established. Still, however, it remained a small and pretty squalid country town.

Ralph Allen, one of Bath's richest citizens is usually credited with the marketing concept of a Bath as a greatly enlarged city of formal architectural beauty which would attract Polite Society. He is credited with discovering John Wood the Elder and giving him the chance of realising his visions of planting a classical city of antiquity on the banks of the Avon. And shrewdly, he encouraged Wood and other builder-architects who followed, to use the Bath stone from his own quarries in ways which showed off its best qualities. The new Bath was a living and evolving sales catalogue for Ralph Allen's Bath Stone.

A great deal has been written about the Georgian architecture of Bath. The formal architecture of the public buildings and the richness of the crescents and squares of new housing provided the perfect foil for the social world which Beau Nash had encouraged. The metamorphosed Bath reflected and flattered the aristocratic society which came there. It too was confident, extravagant, opinionated, cruel, indifferent, snobbish. It was a vast country house set in formal gardens without the visitor having the responsibility of the upkeep during the year. It was a city of palaces; an imitation capital.

"As to the Town you may figure it to yourself by supposing Cavendish Square, Portman Square, and Portland Place, communicating with each other by intermediate streets, and forming a little City," wrote Mrs. Elizabeth Montagu, a regular visitor — a City State, which like its Greek original owed its prosperity at least in part, to sugar and slavery. All those glutted in the successful commercial wars came here, the Admirals to spend their prize-money, the merchants and the ship-builders their profits, the lawyers their fees, the gentry their rents. This was Bath's dilemma — laid out as an aristocratic resort, an 18th century Davos or Montego Bay — it nevertheless attracted the minor gentry and the rich commoners, together with all the fashionable artists, entertainers, tricksters, and tradesmen, so that while it never became an exclusively aristocratic resort, it nevertheless became the national centre and rallying point of Fashion and Polite Society. Beau Nash's rich and booted farmer may have been forbidden the dance floor, but he still visited the King's Bath, rubbed shoulders with an Earl or two, and shared the same dirty water.

The very accessibility of high society at Bath and other watering places was especially tempting to all those who were on the make socially.

The Sweet Ayre of England

Toby Smollett, sometime apothecary's apprentice, surgeon's-mate, novelist, was certainly a man on the make. He spent years at Bath trying to establish himself as a fashionable physician and even wrote a learned paper on the virtue of Hot Waters. The visitors to Bath did not take to him, though God knows there were less qualified men, and some really dangerous quacks whom they did accept. Smollett gave Bath up, his observations put to better use in his satirical masterpiece *Humphrey Clinker*. But Smollett had another disadvantage. He was one of those hungry and footsore Scotsmen who came down to London with their cleverness, their superior education and eagerness to please, to take the jobs of southerners. They were the subjects of a fierce and irrational discrimination and found it easier to volunteer for tough colonial postings, or take jobs as clerks or overseers on the plantations than to slave at home. Smollett had a medical training of sorts in Glasgow, then the most up and coming medical school, and hoped to get a physician's post. All he could manage, however, was an appointment as surgeon's mate on H.M.S. Chichester, a large warship forming part of Admiral Vernon's expedition against the Spanish Main in the dubious so-called War of Captain Jenkin's Ear. The Navy was particularly corrupt and its administrators inept. As one contemporary Admiral said, his ships were "first manned by violence and maintained by cruelty". The conditions on board ship were deplorable, the troops were cramped and ill-fed; the crew was brutalised. When the planned assault on the fortress-port of Carthagena was made, the military leaders were at odds with the navy men and the affair was bungled. Thousands died uselessly from disease and inefficiency, were forced to work in the tropics and, as Smollett wrote later, "sweating under the sun, which was vertical, and fed with putrid beef, rusty pork and bread swarming with maggots". Nevertheless, Admiral Vernon made a great fortune out of the war, accepted the Freedom of the City of London from its grateful merchants and retired to a sinecure directorship, from which he was able to pay frequent and leisurely visits to Bath.

While the fleet anchored at Jamaica, Smollett met his future wife, Anne Lassells. She was a planter's daughter, with expectations of inheriting, so he could expect "a comfortable though moderate estate in that island" as he wrote later. Where other Scots had made their fortunes in well considered West Indian marriages, Smollett was ill-fated. His life was always to be dogged by worries of money, his wife's West Indian income never arrived in time, his mother-in-law was difficult, the problems of the absentee proprietor beyond his solving. His correspondence is an agony of money troubles. To his medical friend William Hunter in 1751:

> I have been hedging and lurching these six weeks in expectation of that cursed ship from Jamaica, which is at last arrived without Letter or Remittance . . .

To another friend, Dr. George Macauley, November 1754:

> Never was I so much harassed with Duns as now; a Persecution which I owe to the Detention of that Remittance from Jamaica which I have expected every day since last Christmas, upon the faith of promises sent from time to time . . .

To his printer, William Strahan, in October 1757:

> It is a very hard case that I should be troubled with Duns for very small sums when there are actually fifteen hundred pounds Sterling at the most moderate Computation due to us at Jamaica . . .

From an early age, he had written, and now he wrote fast and desperately to earn a living. It was hard. He attacked the social order in merciless satires. Society hit back by ignoring him, or gaoling him for libel. He replied by changing his targets. Where Hogarth painted story pictures, Smollett wrote pictures in words. The pretensions of society at Bath, and in particular the nouveau riche visitors from the colonies invited his attack, put into the mouth of his characters. Matthew Bramble, the choleric hypochondriac sees Bath as a microcosm of disorder.

> Every upstart of fortune, harnessed in the trappings of the mode, presents himself at Bath, as in the very focus of observation. Clerks and factors from the East Indies, loaded with the spoil of plundered provinces; planters, negro-drivers and hucksters from our American plantations, enriched they know not how; agents, commissaries and contractors, who have fattened in two successive wars, on the blood of the nation; usurers, brokers and jobbers of every kind; men of low birth and no breeding have suddenly found themselves translated into a state of affluence, unknown to former ages; and no wonder that their brains should be intoxicated with pride, vanity and presumption. Knowing no other criterion of greatness, but the ostentation of wealth, they discharge their affluence without taste or conduct, through every channel of the most absurd extravagance; and all of them hurry to Bath; because here, without any further qualification they can mingle with the princes and nobles of the land.

The Sweet Ayre of England

He goes to an Assembly and faints at the smell,

> It was indeed a compound of villainous smells, in which the most violent stinks and the most powerful perfumes contended for the mastery. Imagine to yourself a high exalted essence of mingled odours arising from putrid gums, imposthumated lungs, sour flatulencies, rank arm-pits, sweating feet, running sores and issues; plaster, ointments and embrocations, Hungary water, spirit of lavender, arsafoetida, drops, musks, hartshorn, and sal volatile; Such O Dick is the fragrant ether we breathe in the polite assemblies of Bath . . .

And as for the architecture:

> The Circus is a pretty bauble, contrived for shew, and looks like Vespasian's amphitheatre turned outside in . . .

and the soft and agreeable valley climate most visitors praise:

> here we valetudinarians pant and struggle, like so many Chinese gudgeons, gasping in the bottom of a punchbowl. . .

and Smollett the failed physican seeing the last possible clients finish the season and leave:

> Not a soul is seen in this place, but a few broken-winded parsons, waddling like so many crows along the North Parade.

Bath, as well as Portman Square, had its Jamaican musicians. Bramble is pestered by the black attendants of a visiting Colonel who insist on practising their French Horns in the hallway, and there are of course West Indian heiresses:

> The ball was opened by a Scotch Lord, with a mulatto heiress from St. Christophers . . .

It is quite surprising that in this crowded and credulous city Smollett was unable to make money.

When Nash died, his regime began to crack. The more crowded Bath became, the more diluted became the cream of society at the top. Bath was taken over by families and friends of people like John Baker.

John Baker, who went to St. Christophers in 1740, is one of the few West Indians whose private family diary, running from 1751 to 1759, has survived. During that period, he and his family are frequently in England, two sons are sent to school, and the Bakers visit Bath and Tunbridge Wells. Here the diary shows that they formed their own social circle with other West Indians with whom they were linked by marriage, by trade, or neighbourhood. The same names that occur and recur in island social activities are prominent in Bath. Here we find the Akerses, the Bannisters, the Douglases, the Ottleys, the Skeretts and the Tuites, the Kirwans, the Phippses and Olivers as well as near relations, the Mannings, who are also big city merchants and shipowners. From Baker's diary it is clear that they play a lot of cards but for low stakes, socialise voraciously, attend balls, concerts and the theatre frequently when in England, and drink the water for its general good effect rather than to remedy any specific ill. In effect, Bath to them is a change of climate and an opportunity for healthy entertainment.

Certainly the Baker family enjoyed Bath. As Solicitor General of the Leeward Islands, John Baker was able to afford a certain style of living, sending his sons to Winchester and Eton, and bringing with him to England on all his visits, his own private slave Jack Beef, who undertook various indispensable duties such as dressing turtles and riding to the hounds with his master.

Such a family connection as the Bakers and their Leeward Island relations, together with their children and servants, their own horses and black slave attendants, would form a very considerable block booking in the season of any watering place, perhaps from 100 to 150 individuals. Similar parties came from Barbados, Antigua and Jamaica to create an overwhelming clientele, not only for lodgings but for houses — houses with stables to accommodate their horses and carriages.

To exploit this situation Sir William Pulteney, a Scottish peer with extensive West Indian estates, bought the Bathwick Estate, just over the river from Bath, intending to build a stately new town development to cater for the floods of visitors. Adam was commissioned to build a bridge — his only commission in the City. The bridge led up a new street of fine shops and houses to Sydney Gardens, Bath's answer to London's Vauxhall and Ranelagh. They were immediately successful, but they accelerated the change in Bath's clientele. More and more towards the turn of the century, the pensioners of modest means were settling here, those who might aspire to, but could not afford, country estates — people like Jane Austen, for "if adventures will not befall a young lady in her own village, she must seek them abroad", and Fanny Burney who had seen Court life, but was forced to live on a small pension.

The Sweet Ayre of England

I wish to live at Bath, wish it devoutly ... London will only do for those who have two houses and of the real country I may say the same ... Bath, therefore, as it eminently agrees with us all, is, in England, the only place for us, since here, all the year round, there is always town at command, and always the country for prospect, exercise and delight.

For the white Jamaicans who could not, for one reason or another, make the cruelly long journey back to England, there remained a small consolation. A mineral spring was discovered in a hilly location and it was quickly turned into a watering place also called Bath. Lady Nugent, the American wife of the British Commander-in-Chief visited it and wrote about it in her diary.

Set off for Bath immediately after breakfast, with an immense cavalcade of gentlemen on horseback, or in Kittareens, sulkies etc. in addition to our own party ... A most beautiful and romantic drive over mountains, on the ledges of precipices, through fertile vallies etc. Bath is a truly lovely village at the bottom of an immense mountain. The houses are surrounded with gardens and cocoa-nut trees ... General N. came at 4. Dined at 6. Mr. Cuthbert and Mr. Chief Justice are here for the waters.

The social amenities were completely lacking, but to have a Bath of sorts in Jamaica must have been a consolation.

8

Pennants on the Roof

The Roman road from Chester to Segontium on the Gwynedd coast opposite the southern tip of Anglesey which followed an uneasy course between the abrupt and rocky mountains and the treacherous coastal marshes, may have been good enough for a swift campaign by the XXth Legion against the Celtic chieftains, but, after 1200 years of neglect, it was hopelessly inadequate as a major artery for trade, social contact or Govenment in a Britain striving towards an industrial society. Yet, up to the mid 18th century, this was the only road, apart from drovers' track and bridle paths, to travel by, in and out of Caernarvonshire. So Caernarvon remained a social and economic backwater of Britain — deprived of leadership because of absentee estate holders; its farms mediaeval; its cattle well adapted to wind and rain, but not to the market; its primitive industries without tools or transport or organisation.

One family, the Pennants, and mainly one man in that family, Richard Penhant, were the means by which the Industrial Revolution came to Caernarvon. They built roads, were great agricultural improvers, planted forests, and above all, used their capital, earned in the first place on their Jamaican sugar plantations to establish and effectively run a major slate industry in North Wales. The story is one of the clearest examples we have of how West Indian riches were the direct catalyst of a major industrial development.

The Pennants were an old Flintshire family, one branch of which produced the antiquary and traveller Thomas Pennant, while another branch had gone fortune hunting in the West Indies. By the mid 18th century, the West Indian Pennants had become one of the most powerful planter families in Jamaica, linked by inter-marriage with the Beckfords, the Longs, the Dawkins, the Morants and the Swymmers, to form a powerful cousinhood with its influence felt in trade and politics, both in Jamaica and in Britain.

John Pennant — father of Richard — left his Jamaica estates and returned to England, sometime in the 1750s. He had a very considerable fortune from his own plantations, plus those of the heiress he had married. Sugar prices were soaring and he was enjoying a growing income in addition to his large capital. He was powerfully connected, and like many of his colleagues he was prepared to use his connection and his capital to raise his own social status, and with it his family's. His elder brother was already in England, an influential man in the City and elected Lord Mayor in 1749. His son Richard had received a Cambridge education and was also now in London working on the family's account and taking an active part in national politics.

In 1761 Richard married Anne, the daughter and heiress of General Hugh Warburton, the Cheshire joint owner of the Penrhyn Estate in Caernarvonshire. John Pennant secured the reversion of the Warburton portion of the estate and negotiated for the other half from the Yonge family, who lived in Devon. Neither of the joint owners had been living on the estate, employing an agent for such slate mining as existed — a virtually static local trade — and for caring for the widely-spread small tenant farmers.

In the first place it was father John who began to exploit the estate to make money. The Pennants had, of course, a wide experience of large scale agriculture in Jamaica with slave labour. Sugar-making would have taught them about the organisation and marketing and transport problems of industry, and their involvement in the Liverpool merchant house which bought and sold on their behalf gave them the experience they were able to use in the slate industry. In Jamaica they had large numbers of cattle and other livestock, together with forests of building timber which gave them a wide overview of agricultural techniques.

The position they found was discouraging. An old mansion, dating from the Tudor period, and badly in need of repair and modernising; the slate quarries pitted with small claims where groups of self-employed quarrymen worked on their own account, paying a royalty on their production; no means of transport except pack horses; virtually no sales beyond the immediate area; the farming land windswept and waterlogged; no attempt at any of the new rotation methods with root crops; stocks of trees in bad shape; tenants with poor morale.

Things were no better along the coast, or at any other of the big Caernarvon estates which had absent owners. At first the Pennants' influence was gradual. John formed the quarrymen into sets or companies, who were made to pay fixed rents instead of royalties on cut slate, and a new slate reeve was appointed to look after the sales and to keep proper records and accounts. At the same time, a comprehensive survey was made of the whole estate with a view to a large scale development.

The development of Penrhyn really got going when John Pennant died in 1782, and Richard inherited the whole estate, plus his father's very considerable wealth. He had already commissioned Samuel Wyatt, one of the numerous architectural Wyatts, to extend and improve the old Hall, and as soon as the work was done, he and his wife Anne moved in.

The Georgian building boom was at its height in the cities and on the country estates all over the country. Slate was the new industrial product which conformed with the recent safety laws and fitted the taste of clients and architects for a quality, but cheap, roofing material — if it could be made and transported to the customer on a sufficient scale. To meet this challenge was the new owner's first task, and he did it energetically and with the generous commitment of his capital.

He got rid of all the small claim workings and took all the work into his own hands with a salaried force of quarrymen. He negotiated with adjacent leaseholders for their land, so that he could plan his quarries systematically on a much grander scale while bearing in mind long term problems of exhaustion and access. He found a very competent quarry manager in James Greenfield, who had great gifts for overcoming past errors and planning for a large scale future. He found locally a slate reeve of unusual talent and ability who not only kept immaculate records and books, but had a gift for labour relations. Houses were built for employees which set a new standard in worker housing of the time. The quay at Abercegin was turned into a port able to berth ocean-going vessels and a new road constructed from Port Penrhyn, as it was now called, to the quarry, capable of taking horsedrawn trucks of slates without loss through breakage.

At the same time, other parts of the estate were being tackled. An ambitious programme of tree planting was begun which continued uninterruptedly to the end of the century, at the average rate of 35,000 trees a year. Cattle and other improved livestock were bred for meat. Tenant farmers were given new leases in which good husbandry and modern methods were rewarded.

All this was planned with great energy and intelligence, it

represented a very considerable outlay of capital, and it was financed from Pennant's own resources. This makes him a very unusual man. At a time when unattached capital was scarce, the actions of anyone who not only had it but was prepared to risk it in a new enterprise, was particularly note-worthy. In the period of which we are writing, neither income tax nor death duties on private wealth existed, so profits and rents could accumulate. On the other hand, the Limited Liability Company in which the investor was only liable in the case of debt for the amount he invested, did not then exist. A bad business could swallow the whole of a person's private fortune, and it often did. The risks of investment were spectacular and personal.

The Pennants had shown that ruthless streak of acquisitiveness which is the mark of the successful entrepreneur in their Jamaican enterprises. In less than three generations the family had acquired very extensive estates and sugar plantations, inter-married with the most influential island families and accumulated a personal fortune. But it was unusual to find the go-getting qualities of one generation being carried into the next, once the fortune was acquired. It is much more usual to find that fortune being squandered by the sons or daughters. Richard's enterprise from this point of view is extraordinary. Brought up at private school and finished at Cambridge, he will have enjoyed the comfort and luxury of a young gentleman of quality, without incentive to effort. Nevertheless, by the age of 23, we find him actively engaged in Parliament in the Beckford interest, marrying shrewdly and working effectively in the family business. In later life he was just as active. His peerage as Lord Penrhyn, given him in 1783, was on the recommendation of Fox for political services. He spoke frequently in the House, especially on the Liverpool trade matters and those affecting the West Indies. Because of his vigorous defence of West Indies interests at the time of Pitt's Irish proposals, he was known as "Chairman of the West India Merchants", and he actually was for a time Chairman of the West India Committee. In 1787 one of the first transport ships to Botany Bay in Australia was named Lady Penrhyn, and was, we must suppose, owned by one of Lord Penrhyn's companies.

His marriage, though apparently successful, was childless and yet the energetic development of the Penrhyn Quarries is a feature of his later life, and one does not know what personal motives directed his untiring efforts to make the slate business succeed.

By 1790 Penrhyn was shipping over three million slates a year, and the other smaller quarries to the west, had been encouraged, or forced to modernise, in order to compete. The whole of the area was feeling the pulse of new economic developments and of ploughed back earnings.

In 1793 the war with France brought with it a bad trade recession. Building investment dropped and so did the demand for slate. To make matters worse, the Government placed a War Tax on slates carried around the coast by sea. This was an unavoidable burden for Penrhyn because of its geographical location — no other transport was economically viable.

Lord Penrhyn was forced to reduce his labour force as the war continued, but used the time to prepare for what he believed was inevitable — a building boom following the end of hostilities. Port Penrhyn was enlarged to allow it to handle larger ships. The horse and cart roadway between the quarry and the Port was replaced by an iron tramway using horsepower. The quarry was comprehensively replanned in terraces which made possible greater productivity, less waste and direct access to the new tramway system.

Penrhyn's vision was completely vindicated in 1801 when a kind of patched up peace of sorts came to the European powers in the so-called Peace of Amiens. Trade in slate for building rose rapidly; in addition there was a new demand for writing slates for schools for which Penrhyn had a virtual monopoly. Apart from coastal trading to Liverpool and London, there was also now a substantial export business with Holland and with the West Indies and demand began to exceed supply.

Richard Pennant's achievements were considerable, but we have not mentioned one essential characteristic. Despite his utterly modern approach to industrial development in Caernarvon, his apparently benevolent and certainly commonsense dealings with his work people and his farming tenants, he remained to the end a die-hard slave owner in the West Indies and a vigorous speaker on behalf of the slave trade. A member of the Jamaica cousinhood, he added his family influence to the strong pressure group in the House of Commons throughout the whole period, from his first election in 1761 to his death. He spoke frequently in the House against Abolition and indeed any attempt to hurt the slave trade.

There was, for instance, a debate on this trade when Liverpool merchants and burgesses presented a Petition to the House of Commons for the uninterrupted continuation of the slave trade of which they had some 60% of the British total. Pennant is reported by Wraxall in his Parliamentary memoirs as being with his fellow Liverpool M.P. Bamber Gascoyne, "The only two Members who volunteered to speak in extenuation, if not justification of the Africa trade . . . and loudly called for an immediate investigation as the sole mode of exposing the calumnies circulated respecting the merchants as well as the planters".

Again, in 1789 on May 12th, he told the House of Commons that "if they passed the vote of Abolition they actually struck at seventy millions of property, they ruined the colonies, and by destroying an essential nursery of seamen, gave up dominance of the sea at a single glance."

He was prominent in the meetings of the London assemblies of merchants and planters throughout the latter part of the 18th century which eventually formalised itself into the West India Committee and he was for some years its Chairman and therefore a key figure in the successful campaign against the Abolitionists led by the West India Committee which helped to delay the end of slavery in the British Empire until 1833.

"The object of emigrants to the West Indies," wrote Lord Brougham in 1803 "is not to live, but to gain — not to enjoy but to save — not to subsist in the colonies, but to prepare for shining in the mother country." If this was the object of the Pennant family it was certainly achieved. Without their wealth and initiative, one valuable breakthrough in the Industrial Revolution would not have taken place and Caernarvon itself might have remained as Connemara remains to this day, an undeveloped and blighted county with its people trapped in a feudal past.

In 1808 Richard Pennant died, and the Irish peerage became extinct. His widow carried on the business until she too died in 1815. There were no children or near relations, so the estate and the family fortune went to a nephew George Hay Dawkins, another very wealthy Jamaican planter who had chosen to live in England.

George Hay Dawkins was a limb of another powerful Jamaican sugar planting clan whose increasingly sophisticated tastes and social ambitions had turned into absentee proprietors.

One of George's uncles, James Dawkins, became a passionate gentleman archeologist of classic sites in Greece and Asia Minor. He was an early member of the prestigious Society of Dilettanti — the eighteenth century club for rich collectors and cognoscenti — and he helped by his presence and his money, the architects Stuart and Revett to make their painstaking and influential recording of the great buildings of Athens.

James' brother Henry, had ambitions which were more conventional for the period, that is to "shine" as a country gentleman and as an M.P. Settling in the West Country he first took his seat in the Commons for Southampton in 1761 in the Beckford Interest. A few years later he bought the marvellously sited estate

95

and house called Standlynch overlooking the River Avon south of Salisbury. Here, using his Jamaican income, he set in train an ambitious building programme to transform the large country house into a superbly elegant but enormous mansion. His architects were Revett and John Wood the younger of Bath, both friends of his brother James, using as models some of the elements from the great Greek masterpieces they had surveyed years previously. Henry indeed shared his brother's tastes.

But Henry Dawkins had no family and while he lived to enjoy the house and grounds for many years, as an exercise in putting down grandiose family roots, it was a dead end. When he died in 1814, the mansion was bought by a grateful nation for the heirs and successors of Lord Nelson.

It was now up to nephew George to scale the final peaks of Dawkins pretensions. This he did in a thoroughly unorthodox fashion. He inherited from his uncles' estates in Jamaica, and he inherited the Penrhyn Quarries with the huge mountain estates and the Penrhyn family mansion. He found the slate quarries and the agricultural development of the estate both profitable and advanced in their technology. But he found the house little altered by his predecessors, its best feature the wild and awe-inspiring views over the Bay of Beaumaris and up the Snowdonian massif.

Basically it was still an old Tudor brick house of some pretension — a clerical manse for a future Archbishop of York in the 17th century — patched up and modified over its long life, but essentially the heavy mullioned and ivy covered squire's house of the period. Years of neglect from absentee owners and tenants had done nothing for its comfort and amenity. The view was its chief glory and its isolation, neither of which were fashionable until the Romantics held sway in matters of taste.

Richard and Anne Pennant apparently did not mind. Certainly they made some improvements to comfort, but the shell of the house remained the same. There must have been reasons, but since they have left no memoirs or letters, we can only guess at them. First, both of them were political animals. Richard was one of the two Liverpool M.P's from 1767 to 1780 and from 1784 to 1790 and had to spend a good deal of time in London. She was an energetic canvasser and vote getter; he was a regular speaker in the House of Commons. We know that he made at least thirty speeches in the House between 1784 and 1790, all on matters of Liverpool trade or the West Indies. Second, we know that the Pennant's energies were absorbed in the enormous work of regenerating the Penrhyn estate, both in an agricultural sense and by building up a new industry in slate. Thirdly, whatever the reasons, the couple remained childless. There was no pressure to create a bigger, more convenient home for a growing family. Fourthly, they were cut off geographically from the demands of society and the need to impress by ostentatious show. Their personal lives appear to have been frugal and austere. Anne would no doubt have accompanied her husband to London, and they kept another house there. They also kept a house at Winnington in Cheshire, the ancient seat of the Pennants and a more practical base for business in Liverpool. George might not inherit the Penrhyn peerage but he could attach the Pennant interest by taking the family name and adding it to his own.

Dawkins Pennant, luckily for the slate industry, was also an energetic and able businessman. Under his leadership the Penrhyn quarries' output went up to 25,000 tons a year and the labour force to 900 men. He continued his cousins's road building programme with a daring road from the coast and Bethesda to Capel Curig in the heart of the mountains and made it possible for a new main road from the Midlands to Holyhead and Ireland to be planned and built on to it. The grandeur and epic scenery of Snowdonia was opened up to tourists who had drunk at the fountain of such Romantic poets and painters as Wordsworth, Byron, Turner and Richard Wilson. Trade and industry benefitted equally.

The Pennants and Dawkin's West Indian fortunes certainly gave North Wales a serious economic and social boost and a part in the Industrial Revolution, but there is another and more frivolous reason why the inheriting Dawkins is remembered. It is for the huge pseudo-Norman castle which he built at Penrhyn to replace the old family hall. If it had been built by negro slaves imported from Jamaica, we could not be more astonished than we are by this enduring and eccentric monument to an obsession — for obsession is the only possible reason for such a place. No glib remarks about nouveau riche planters seeking to ape and surpass their aristocratic betters will do either, for Dawkins, or for his equally amazing contemporary and cousin, William Beckford of Fonthill Abbey. Beckford had a dream of towers, towers in which he could live a solitary and luxurious existence. Dawkins had a more robust dream, that of a latter-day Norman Baron, sallying forth from his fine protective citadel to survey his hides and his peasants, looking out from the battlements of his lofty Keep across the waters to Beaumaris Castle with its concentric defences and sea wall; sitting in his great hall throwing bones to his dogs and waited on by armies of servants; staring up at the rugged rainswept crags of Gwynedd pondering a daring strategy for smoking out a Welsh resistance force. And he made his dream come true.

Thomas Hopper, an able and eclectic architect who had already a reputation in the fashionable West End, where gentlemen, retiring early from the political skirmishing at Westminster for the more exhilarating activity of cards or billiards in their St. James clubs would be conscious of his improvements at Arthur's, now the Carlton Club, and of his commission for the Prince Regent at Carlton House Terrace for a conservatory. Dawkins Pennant commissioned him to design and build his new mansion and appears to have given him freedom, both with his bank account, and his imagination. The work took ten years. The result was a gigantic and imposing neo-Norman castle with a Victorian stroke or two, a kind of Arundel Castle in corsets, ramrod stiff and elbows in on its stark landscape setting. No jerry-built sham this — architectural critics all agree it works surprisingly well, and it still stands under the protection of the National Trust for all of us who can still dream, to visit and enjoy. But if the exterior is impressive, the interiors are even more so. The great hall is the chief tour de force, floored with polished slate from the Penrhyn quarries and the design and scale of it is copied from the transept at Durham Cathedral. This was after all, the great age of plasterwork and Hopper's own decoration in all the public rooms is vastly extravagent and even frenzied. The mediaeval atmosphere is carried through the decor into the furniture itself with the use of Mona marble from Anglesey, a great deal of slate and oak from the estate, even to the creation of a special slate bed weighing over four tons which immediately became a curiosity and talking point for all visitors. It is reported that Queen Victoria resisted the invitation to sleep in it on a royal visit. Hopper even designed suitable Norman furniture to sit on the black polished slate. All the interiors were on a vast and opulent scale and even the stables big enough to house today a large collection of industrial steam locomotives.

Was Penrhyn only a dream solidly fleshed out with the aid of a bottomless bank balance, or was there more to it?

By the time of Hopper's commission, the reaction against the classical elegance of the Georgian style was gaining impetus. The Romantic movement and its bizarre off-shoot the Gothic Revival were rapidly gaining ground.

At the beginning of the 18th century — the Augustan age of literature and art — people of taste and education looked back with a shudder at all that preceded the Reformation. Mediaeval was a term of reproach. The period which attracted them was that which marked the highest achievement of the human mind, combined with a natural elegance of building and art — the ancient Greek civilisation and its reflection in the Italian Renaissance. For most of the 18th century the acme of good taste was a Palladian mansion in strict imitation of classic proportion and style and as the Adam town house with its symmetry and discreet, almost monotonous repetition of fine decoration, white panelled rooms, gay striped wallpapers and flimsy furniture. In our increasingly ugly and overcrowded environment, we look back on the period as a Golden Age of graceful living, hoping not to be reminded of the unspeakable squalor and violence of everyday life which was the inescapable element of all 18th century existence.

It was not long before the rich and literate people who lived in these agreeable Georgian residences tired of them and began to yearn for something less well ordered, less imitative. As early as 1747, Horace Walpole, eccentric wit and memoirist, bought a villa at Strawberry Hill in Surrey which he began to Gothicise.

"Every true Goth", wrote Walpole, "must perceive that the rooms are more the work of fancy than of imitation".

Walpole's position in high society, combined with his reputation as extravagent raconteur and wealthy wit ensured the maximum publicity for his villa. Strawberry Hill combined as many mediaeval elements as possible — battlements, tracery, ceilings copied from Gothic cathedrals, dark and glowing tapestries and hangings, suits of armour on the staircase — without allowing them to disturb the way of life preferred by an 18th century man of taste and breeding.

It is generally accepted now that Walpole was not the originator of the Gothic Revival. The idea was in the wind, he caught it and gave it his own particular twist, and became its most potent catalyst. Absorbing the atmosphere and excitement of his own creation, Walpole was inspired to write *The Castle of Otranto*, the first Gothic tale of mystery and horror. It was the precursor of a stream of Gothic romances which the novel buying public eagerly collected and read in their spacious well-ordered salons and withdrawing rooms, slaking the thirst of their over-disciplined and mannered minds with visions of secret passages, dark and dreadful dungeons, chatelaines menaced by mad monks, blood on the cold stone and owls hooting mysteriously from the tops of ruined towers. Soon these good people required more concrete stimulants for their imaginations and the passion for mock ruins and Gothic summer houses began. Gothic fantasy has been a powerful inspiration in the culture of the Western world ever since, emerging here in literature, there in architecture, now in film, feeding on fashions for the sadistic, sexually inspired evil, and the supernatural.

Some of these elements may well have influenced Dawkins Pennant and his architect Hopper in deciding on the form and atmosphere of the new mansion.

The boom years for Gothic and other mediaeval fortifications on private mansions were still ahead, but the restoration of Gothic cathedrals and interest in new neo-Gothic churches was in full swing and with this more direct attraction for the past, came an obsession with ancestry and roots.

William Beckford was obsessed with genealogy and spent lavishly trying to establish a hereditary link for himself with Edward III. The heraldic devices invented or claimed by him were a potent motif in the decorative surfaces of Fonthill Abbey, and attracted one of William Cobbett's better jibes:

> Talking of Normans and high blood, puts me in mind of Beckford and his "Abbey"! The public knows that the tower of this thing fell down some time ago. It was built of Scotch fir and cased with stone! In it there was a place which the owner had named "The Gallery of Edward III, the frieze of which", says the account, "contains the achievements of seventy-eight Knights of the Garter, from whom the owner is lineally descended"! Was there ever vanity and impudence equal to these! The negro-driver brag of his high blood! . . .

To cap it all, Walter Scott's *Ivanhoe*, one of that prolific best-seller's most popular novels, was published in 1819. It was, of course, a rumbustious tale of Norman and Saxon rivalry, of noble and ignoble deeds, of feasts in great tapestry bedecked halls, of tournaments against the backdrop of hoary and ancient castles with their looming donjons and wellguarded barbicans. All the panoply of chivalry, the challenge of knight to knight, claimant and disclaimant, of inheritor and disinheritor. And for the reader tuned in on the right wavelength like George Hay Dawkins Pennant, the image of four black slaves building the bonfire on which the Jewess Rebecca is to be unjustly burnt for witchcraft. Anachronistic perhaps, but a touch to which no West Indian could have failed to respond.

It is most unlikely that Dawkins Pennant would have been immune to the attractions of ancestry. After all, he was fresh from Jamaica, not even second generation, and his social standing would be endangered accordingly. If Beckford could create such roots, why shouldn't he. He was after all, a member of the once-powerful cousinhood. Some such idea was certainly behind his adopting the Pennant name on to his own, a popular device for establishing family right, and his concern is demonstrated by an eagerness to inherit the Barony of Penrhyn given to Richard Pennant in 1783 for political services and dormant since his death. This he eventually achieved, exerting all his business, political and new social status, in 1820. So it is a reasonable deduction that establishing a respectable, if bogus ancestry, was behind Dawkins Pennant's Norman boast as well.

And merely the site itself, made its contribution. Rich in historical association, lashed by the elements from sea on the North and mountain from the South, unparalleled views, the needs of a chief amongst men in taming a wild frontier, all must have contributed to the idea of some kind of castellated residence. And with Beaumaris Castle over the water, Conway to the East and Caernarvon to the West, Penrhyn Castle almost begins to look inevitable.

The second Lord Penrhyn was obviously happy with it, and from it he presided over the continuing success of the great Penrhyn slate industries and the development of Caernarvon as a modern community. West Indian money had strongly fertilised one part of Britain that conventional methods of growth might never have reached.

9

All That We Can Rap and Rend

The strongest image that one gets from reading the scattered fragments of letters and accounts of the 18th century West India merchants is that of a bunch of pirates who, in a series of swift costume changes, slip off their eye patches and their cutlasses, exchanging them fast for the quill and contracts of the honest broker and then the furs and gold chains of high office. In the former they stand on the plundering frontier of Empire, in the latter they stand four square at the centre of'England's most hallowed business and civic institutions. They change their clothes, but do they change their minds? My feeling is that they do not, they simply become master of another disguise. One or two examples illustrate this.

In the early years of the British settlement of the West Indian islands there were, very broadly speaking, only two classes of settler. There were the planter masters who might be gentlemen of resource, or yeomen with a few saved pounds, and there were servants. Servants included all artisans, tradesmen, as well as general field hands, or domestic servants. All lived close to their respective masters in primitive hutments around the fringes of the would-be plantation, or in the case of the bigger planters, under the lee of his master's fortified house, built to provide protection against attack from Caribs, pirates, or even his own disatisfied servants. There were no towns, perhaps only a few watch huts at the most suitable landing site. Towns were indeed actively discouraged as being against the best interests of the home country. They might encourage trades and manufactures to compete with English goods, an unthinkable crime. But as tropical crops flourished and sugar planting advanced, so the number of ships plying back and forth across the Atlantic increased, and it was no longer possible to work off the foreshore, lifting each individual hogshead of sugar or molasses into a rowing boat and paddling it out to the ship in the anchorage. So primitive dock facilities grew up and around them the services which accompany shipping trades wherever they flourish — warehousing, shipwrights, inns, brothels, money-exchangers. Father Biet, who was in Barbados in 1654, describes the growth of Bridgetown, the island's future capital, "The town is built along a section of the port. It carries the name of Bridge. There are easily three or four hundred houses which are all inns or stores filled with goods. All the houses are built of timber and boards." Where inn-keepers flourished, shop-keepers soon followed and the tradesmen who supplied the goods for both. The tide of trade was unstoppable. Several important London merchants who were investors in planting ventures were not slow to see the advantages of having their own agents on the islands, to buy and also to sell. Planters with relatives in trade back home requested cargoes of suitable goods and went into wholesale trading on their own account. As the population and wealth of the plantations grew, so did the demand for goods to provide a better standard of living. A new breed of middleman emerged.

> Hatts, Hose, Shoes, Gloves, Swords, Knives, Locks, Keys etc. Victuals of all kinds, that will endure the sea, in so long a voyage. Olives, Capers, Anchoves, salted Flesh and Fish, pickled Maquerells and Herrings, Wine of all sorts, and the boon Beer d'Angleterre.

In the sweltering tropics the demand for drink was enormous, especially for wines and spirits which could stand the long sea voyage. Not only did the planters have an unquenchable thirst which is frequently referred to by the chroniclers, but the thirst of visiting sailors was also prodigious.

Where he originally came from, we have no idea, but before the turn of the century, Edward Lascelles was selling wine from his own wharf at Bridgetown, just like the first Peter Beckford in Jamaica, and performing certain useful services in the way of providing credit and cash for British warships on station in the Caribbean. It is possible he may already have had experience in acting as a factor for slaves, and that his father had built up a trading connection before him. His brother Henry too, was also living on the island before 1714 and is referred to in official papers as someone who is "an established person". Henry indeed, married a Barbadian lady, and probably through his friendship with Governor Lowther, became Collector of Customs, one of the most lucrative "places" on the island. Another brother, Philip, is also referred to as, "trading out of London to Barbados" in 1702, and may have been directly concerned with the wine trade, though the connection is by no means certain.

In 1700 Edward came into possession of a substantial sugar plantation and he sat as a member of the Assembly. As his trading connections extended, it became possible to follow the route taken by other ambitious West Indian merchants, the route to bigger and better profits in the commercial capital and to the ease and comfort of life in England as opposed to the unhealthiness and uncertainties of the tropics. The movement of enterprising men back from the islands had become sufficiently noticeable to be deplored. Littleton, himself an ex-Barbadian planter, now an active sugar spokesman in the capital wrote in 1689 . . .

> By a kind of magnetic force England draws to it all that is good in the plantations, It is the center to which all things tend. Nothing but England can we relish or fancy: our hearts are here, wherever our bodies be. If we get a little money, we remit it to England. They that are able, breed up their children in England. All that we can rap and rend is brought to England . . .

Feeling on the island was very mixed about the growing number of absentees. Against the move back to England, it was argued, that it was usually the more vigorous and enterprising citizens who left and they left the government of the island in the hands of less able men and stripped the defence militia of fighters. Their departure exaggerated the ratio of white masters to slaves, it increased the burden of defence and taxation on the remaining planters. Furthermore, the absentees handed their estates into the care of overseers or agents who were less conscientious, often cruel in their management. Slaves, bereft of hope, were more given to insurrection.

In favour of the move back to England, all or any of the following could be argued. That absentees were able to bring influence to bear on Government and trading circles to the benefit of the colonies; that they could effectively counter jealous attempts by competitive trades to undermine their prosperity; that their own experts acting in trade on their behalf would be able to get better terms, better credit, suit their requirements more exactly than those without experience; that they could learn advance information of national policy, naval expeditions, the likelihood of war or the end of it and all things likely to affect the price of sugar which was immensely valuable. But let me not give the impression that all absentees spoke with one voice, far from it. There were indeed issues on which all made common cause, but planters held views often at variance with merchants and both with representations of colonial government. It was not until the end of the 18th century when the threat to the slave trade united them all in a common and opposing front.

The London to which Edward Lascelles returned was a great trading city and a great port. Rapidly rebuilt after the Great Fire it sprawled from Wapping to Tothill Fields, with building developments filling in all the space between the old City and the ancient country villages of Islington, Marylebone, Tottenham, Chelsea. The river was like a floating forest from London Bridge to Blackwall with the overcrowded quays and shipbuilding yards, offices and warehouses of numberless local and international trades, along its banks. Defoe wrote that London was a city that "sucks the vitals of trade in this island to itself". But it was above all, the export centre of England. The Thames provided a safe natural harbour for a very large number of ships, it was conveniently placed for trading to and from the great ports and markets of continental Europe, the principal Naval Dockyards were downstream to provide protection and convoy in time of war. This was the period when war was an aspect of trade. "Where trade is at stake," said Chatham, "you must defend it or perish." The great wars of the period were fought for profit and the undisturbed exclusive right to exploit world markets and colonies. To do this, the British Government deployed the full apparatus of Laws — Navigation Acts to protect its shipping; Staple Acts to protect vital commodities; trading companies operating under exclusive Royal Charters to corner the most precious and profitable trades; the East India Company for the exploitation of India and the Far East; the Royal African Company for the monopoly of the African slave trade. Both these companies had their headquarters and principal trading bases in London.

London was deeply involved in the slave trade and all other aspects of the booming sugar trade with the Caribbean. The Royal African Company had proved itself as ineffective in supplying the slave needs of the expanding plantation economy and by 1700 was facing a full scale attack from merchants anxious to share in the fantastic pickings. The largest London merchants were indeed immensely powerful, a force difficult for the Government to gainsay when united in a common cause. Most Government finance was provided by City loans, the negotiations for which were opportunities of bargaining on a grand and greedy scale. From these encounters, the protagonists of free enterprise

105

capital never came away empty handed.

Opportunity knocked for anyone with vigour and capital. Edward Lascelles had both. He was later joined by brother Henry, who had made a fortune from his customs collectorship in Barbados. Some of Henry's methods had attracted unfavourable attention amongst his political opponents.

One of the favourite ways of building up a swift, but risky fortune, was to deal in smuggled French, Danish or Dutch sugars and rums and ship them into the British market as ordinary colonial crops. Small boats slipped by night into hidden creeks and the goods were transferred first to a plantation and then down to a port where they were cleared to England, or elsewhere as being of local origin, and therefore attracting lower duty. The outsiders enjoyed it because they got a quicker and bigger return than they normally got from their own market, the planter liked it because he could sell it very profitably, and the merchant because he was able to undercut currently quoted prices and attract customers quickly. It was in fact a traffic carried on widely and largely in the open. Henry Lascelles was accused of indulging in this traffic on a large scale and also of adulterating the quality of goods collected in barter payment of customs duty and selling the better goods on his own account. Indeed, as a precaution against prosecution, he immediately sought and bought a seat in the House of Commons, becoming the member for Northallerton, and which he held until he resigned in favour of his son Daniel. To the trading company he brought a great deal of capital which he was willing to risk, and a talent known more for cunning than for candour.

The main activity of the House was sugar factoring, but during the course of two generations, it broadened its scope to include slave factoring, ship-ownership and all kinds of general trading.

The sugar factor's job was to sell his correspondent's sugar, and for doing it, he received a commission — hence commission-agent. In its simplest working, the crop from a given estate was put on board a suitable merchant vessel and delivered to Lascelles, care of the Port of London. When the cargo arrived, the broker paid all the necessary duties out of his own funds, together with the freight charges, wharfage, lighterage, cost of warehousing and all other handling charges. These were then charged to the shipper. The sugars were then sold, commissions calculated and a balance drawn. From the balance the factor bought all the items the planters required from home: barrel hoops, cloth, metal hardware, crockery, furniture, salt, clothes and all kinds -of luxuries — all of course to be procured at the most advantageous prices.

The factor was also expected to be banker of any surplus funds, the political representative in the case of a dispute, procurer of "places" for aspiring relatives, and as guardian of any children sent to England to be educated; and he was frequently asked to provide suitable boys as book-keepers or trainee overseers.

From all this miscellaneous activity carried on, for many correspondents there were several inevitable consequences. The agent was drawn into the shipping trade to carry all these goods here and there. He was drawn into wholesale trading of supplies. He became an expert in terms of insurance and from that it was a small step into the actual insurance business itself. It became cheaper to hold one's own warehouses rather than rent them, and maybe, become one of the few wharfingers along the "legal" quays. For all these activities there were agreed charges or commissions, so even a relatively simple set of transactions would amass a whole number of small profits.

But of course, this simple picture disguises a multitude of difficulties, a consideration of which would be extremely technical and out of place in a book of this nature and there is indeed a great deal of literature on the subject. While sugar prices continued to rise and the factor limited his advances of goods to the planter to a balance with the expected annual cargo of sugar, he was in little risk, he took his percentages off both trades and he became very wealthy, but planters had extraordinary needs for credit, the purchase of slaves for instance, or new equipment for which they needed longer terms. Planters were always capital-hungry and they became, as the 18th century progressed, increasingly in the hands of their agents, many of whom held mortgages on their estates as security and who in bad cases of persistent debt were forced to foreclose.

The really spectacular profits for the West India merchants were however to be made in the slave trade, and the Lascelles engaged in it fully and whole-heartedly at many levels. Barbados was one of the principal slave marts in the Caribbean. It was the first port of call after the Atlantic crossing and almost all captains stopped there to re-provision, ask for news about the state of the market, or to take the earliest opportunity of offering their cargoes for sale. The Lascelles, through their own agents in Barbados, engaged in this trade. As shipowners they invested numerous shares of ships or cargoes in the Guinea trade. In fact they complained that they had so many ships at one time that they got in each others way.

Henry Lascelles was also the chief promoter of a scheme for a floating factory to be anchored off the Gold Coast where goods could be exchanged for slaves as occasion arose and other ships could restock it and remove the assembled slaves. The matter is fully described in a book on *Merchants and Mariners* by Conrad Gill and what emerges from this is that the inhumanity of the slave trade was as widely understood along the Thames and by all those trading in the port as it was in the more obviously brutal and single-minded city of Liverpool. There is the same cast of characters, the good ladies who provide fetters and iron collars, sisters and mothers who take out shares in slaving voyages, captains who double-cross their owners by carrying on their own illicit trade, the blood-lusting young midshipmen only waiting for their superior officers to die so that they can be promoted, not to mention all the tradesmen who put in their cloth, their trinkets, their guns as speculative cargo.

Whatever the House of Lascelles did, however remote in terms of accepting pretty abstract bills of exchange, lending money to planters or to merchants or building ships, it ultimately boiled down to a traffic in slaves.

When Henry made his Will in 1753 shortly before his death, he had £284,000 to divide out, without including annuities. Of this, £53,000 was invested in land in Yorkshire; some £60,000 in public funds and £166,000 to his elder son Edwin, who had never had anything to do with the London business and thus enriched, was able to found an aristocratic family dynasty.

The Lascelles business continued throughout the 18th century as Lascelles and Maxwell and continued into recent times as Wilkinson and Gaviller. Only during the Blitz of 1940 was the old counting house destroyed, and the almost unique files of 17th and 18th century letters and bills lost by fire.

The Lascelles already had a house and park called Gawthorpe near Leeds and when Edwin succeeded in 1754, he commissioned a team of architects and craftsmen to plan and build a great family mansion which could be set off worthily against the palatial house of his political boss the Duke of Rockingham a few miles away at Wentworth Whithouse, one of the most luxurious and imposing of all the grand eighteenth century english houses.

Edwin Lascelles chose as his collaborators John Carr, the Yorkshire stone mason who became a great North Country architect and social luminary, Robert Adam to design the interiors, together with Angelica Kauffmann and Anthonio Zucchi for the decorations. The furniture was to be from the up-and-coming young Chippendale.

The site chosen for the new Harewood House was an impressive one with prospects to the south east and west, and the scale of the house was designed for large public gatherings with the greatest possible care and luxury going into the great public rooms; the gallery seventy-five feet long arranged to display a series of huge Reynolds family portraits, a breathtaking hall leading through into a large salon from which one looked out over a magnificent landscape. It was from end to end an ostentatious though completely tasteful show of wealth and magnificence with which to impress both Court and country.

All the 18th century Lascelles took an active part in politics as M.P.'s and when necessary they all combined on matters of common West Indian interest. As befitted the head of a great land-owning family, Edwin sat as M.P. for Yorkshire and for Northallerton, the family's own seat. In 1790, in consideration of the formidable family interest, he was made Baron Harewood, but leaving no surviving son, was succeeded by his cousin Edward, who later became Viscount Lascelles and the First Earl of Harewood. The family fortunes, now mainly in good English land and safe Government stocks, survived intact the fall of the West Indian sugar market after 1815. The 19th century Earls were handsome, rich, went to Eton and into the Army, were welcome at Court, and did their duty as Yorkshire landowners, caring for their estates. Two of them at least followed each other head first into the next world as a result of a hunting accident.

The sixth Earl, who married the then Princess Royal, died in 1947, and the present Earl, a cousin of the Queen, has broken with the stuffier family traditions by devoting his life and work to the encouragement of the arts, in particular opera and music, to which he has been patron, administrator and an able director of many festivals.

In Barbados, the name of Lascelles is still commemorated in an estate of that name, though it no longer belongs to the family and the Hon. Gerald Lascelles still possesses the estates of The Mount and The Belle.

Cardinal Manning, that epitome of refined religious agony, was the fourth son of the great "Billy" Manning, pillar of the Bank of England and powerful West Indian merchant.

The rise of the Manning family was a swift one. In the days of good Queen Anne, John Manning was a small-time planter on the tiny island of St. Kitts. Profiting both by the defeat of the French by General Codrington and by a clever marriage, he was able to improve his plantation to which his son, William Coventry Manning, added a trading company. He too married a plantation heiress Elizabeth Ryan, and with the accumulated revenue, the

Coventry Mannings were able to move to England, ambitious to trade and live on a grander scale. In this they were quickly successful, aided by the sugar boom which followed the defeat of the French and interruption of their sugar trade in the Seven Years War. Manning, like many other planters and merchants was able to profit by his double involvement as planter and as trader. At first, he and his family lived over their various counting houses in the City, moving from Broad Street to St. Mary's Axe, then out to Edmonton and a large house at Wanstead. In 1778 he bought the prestigious house and estate of Copped Hall at Totteridge in Hertfordshire and lived there until he died. For his two daughters he was able to offer dowries of £15,000 each, which, of course, was a very substantial capital sum indeed, and both girls made good matches. The elder, Elizabeth married a prosperous city merchant with estates in Warwickshire and Sara married John Laurens, the son of Henry Laurens, the President of the American Congress.

The elder son, John, showed no aptitude for business, an 18th century dropout, who might have destroyed the family's growing fortune if he had inherited, but he died before he came of age. The second son William, known as "Billy" to distinguish him for his father, on the other hand displayed remarkable talent in the counting house. Money was indeed a highly respectable driving force in Georgian England, but "Billy" was absorbed in an almost total admiration and obsession with it and its perquisites. His first wife, Elizabeth, was the daughter of Abel Smith, the powerful Nottingham banker who was also closely involved in the development of the Bank of England and other private city banks.

It was the time of great commercial expansion in the City. Private banks had developed as off-shoots of the great merchant houses, employing the massive influx of capital which was the result of British success in colonial wars, first with the Dutch and then with the French. The Bank of England was founded in 1694 by a group of merchants to meet an urgent need for a new method of dealing with increasingly complex Government finance and rapidly grew in power and influence. It was given a monopoly for the issue of bank notes and it discounted Government bills, as well as administering large Loan Stock issues and bonds. Other banks foundered in the rash of wild speculative ventures like the South Sea Company, but the Bank of England was increasingly the rock on which such national scandals broke safely. At the head of the list of stock-holders were most of the English ducal Whig families. Confidence in the Bank extended overseas to attract the funds of foreign companies and Governments. To be part of such a body was a mark of very considerable commercial standing.

"Billy" was already a partner in several of the Manning family West India businesses, and proprietor of his own trading house at 8 Billeter Square, when his father died. He was now one of the City's wealthiest merchants. With his father-in-law's connection he soon became a Director of the Bank of England. He adored the ritual pomp of the Bank and the dignity of becoming a pillar of such an institution. He moved into his father's mansion of Copped Hall and every day he drove to the Bank in grand style, in a lordly carriage-and-four with black postillions and outriders.

His first wife had died without producing an heir, but his second wife presented him in rapid succession with four boys and four girls. Clearly a new role was needed of him. He saw himself as a patriarchal figure, respected and obeyed in all his many activities. In the City his knowledge, his experience and his powerful connections were highly regarded; as a plantation owner he saw himself as the patriarch leading his black children out of an African wilderness into the light, a kindly law-giver, a firm but careful disciplinarian, punishing justly, never cruel. As an M.P. he spoke on behalf of himself and his colleagues with their huge capital investments in the British West Indies and of the glory and grandeur which sugar had brought to England. In a portrait by Lonsdale, he sits enthroned in portly splendour radiating integrity and stability from every pore. In the background radiating golden warmth — the Bank of England. In his domestic life he felt it necessary to project an image of exceptional piety, which one suspects had as much to do with his social aspirations as genuine religious experience. He positively refused to have his children baptized by anyone less than a Bishop, the Church, he considered owed it to his rank and dignity. Yet throughout the period when the humanitarians, including many Evangelical Christians, were contributing weighty and telling arguments to the case for the Abolition of Slavery, "Billy" continued to work and speak vehemently against them and to protest against the efforts of missionaries attempting to Christianise negroes in the West Indies. In this, of course, he conformed to the position on slavery which most members of the Anglican Church, to its everlasting discredit, felt to be reasonable. The Church was convinced that it was perfectly in order to trade in and keep negro slaves, provided they were pagan. Even the Society for the Propagation of the Gospel could keep slaves at work on two plantations given them by Christopher Codrington, while using the revenue from their work to train missionaries to convert other peoples slaves. There was no question of converting their own, because that would endanger their slave status. On practical grounds, the British planter was bound to oppose Christianisation for their slaves, it made them less tractable to discipline and it meant teaching them English, by means of which they could overcome the problems of communication between tribes and perhaps organise themselves into revolt, and so "Billy' Manning strongly opposed Wilberforce's Bill for Abolition in 1796.

At the peak of its prosperity the firm of Manning and Anderson had an income of over £25,000 a year, but after the end of the Napoleonic War, the British West Indian monopoly of the European sugar market was coming to an end, sugar prices fell drastically and both planters who had mortgaged themselves against good future trade, and the commission houses who had agreed to finance their forward needs for equipment, slaves and other supplies, found themselves in deep water. Manning's company was one of them. First he was forced to sell Copped Hall to help maintain the company's credit and move to a smaller country house in Kent, but eventually the sheer weight of failures amongst planters and traders dragged them down and he was declared a bankrupt in 1831. His obituary, written by the future Cardinal said that "he felt the droughts of commercial credit like a wound...".

Of the four sons, William the eldest, died at the age of 19, Frederick entered his father's firm as a partner and lived to the ripe old age of 83 as a bachelor. Charles became Page of Honour to George IV and his son too died a bachelor. Finally, there was Henry Edward, the youngest son, more like his father than any of the others, who, dashed by his father's business failure from the brilliant social and political career to which he aspired, focussed all his prodigious ego, his need of personal ritual, and his thirst for the best society, in becoming, instead, a prince of the Catholic Church.

10

Xanadu of a Wiltshire Hilltop

When Alderman Beckford caught a fatal chill in 1770, his wealth, his family and his network of "interests" made him one of the most powerful individuals of his generation. He owned fourteen sugar plantations in Jamaica with 1,000 slaves and was buying more when he died. His numerous properties in England included a 5,000 acre estate at Fonthill in Wiltshire. He was an M.P., twice Lord Mayor of London, a prominent city merchant, shipowner and dealer.

Dauntless in political controversy, autocratic in business, lusty in life, Beckford was the Godfather of his chosen world. When he died, his one legitimate son William, inherited the bulk of his property and business, but at the age of ten was naturally unable to exercise any strong influence on the direction of so diverse and untidy a property and commercial empire. Nor could he satisfy the expectations of numerous natural sons and daughters on whom the Alderman had lavished love and money when he was alive; nor could he cope with the greed of his father's business agents. For the moment at least, his executors could deal with these problems, and deal with them they did, badly, with the maximum possible recourse to costly litigation and minimum gain to the estate.

The house at Fonthill was now home for young William and his mother. It was huge and empty. When the Alderman bought the estate in 1736, it contained a large country house but this was destroyed by fire in 1755 and was rebuilt on a much more splendid scale. So grand in effect, that it was renamed Fonthill Splendens. A centre block of four stories was approached by two sweeping flights of steps. Further out, two symmetrical wings of two stories completed the house. Inside, the apartments were sumptously decorated. On the ground floor was a huge and fantastic Egyptian Hall, a meeting point of many corridors and an imposing staircase leading up to suites of luxurious apartments. One suite, in Turkish style, had large mirrors and ottomans; all the walls were hung with expensive works of art and every room was packed with sideboards of cabinets full of gold, silver, precious metals, precious stones, ceramics and other opulent finery. In the well-stocked library were illustrated Arabic texts and Chinese erotic art. Such a total display was overwhelming to most visitors but, even in the Alderman's lifetime, there were few.

The traditional landed nobility and local gentry, with some hypocrisy, made the Alderman's dubious morals the excuse for staying away, when they probably simply disliked his success and ostentation, his lack of charm or manners. Beckford was not a man to make himself "amiable", to use the contemporary phrase, nor would a man capable of outfacing the King, as he did over the Wilkes case, have hidden his "uncouth" radical politics from his guests. The huge army of servants may have been kept busy dusting and cleaning, but certainly not waiting on visitors.

Nor did William's mother approve of the house. In marrying the Alderman, she had married beneath her, and she never let anyone forget it. Marriages among people of property were more matters of finance than of love and Maria may have been the widow of another city man, Francis Marsh, but she was also the daughter of the Hon. George Hamilton, a near relation of the Duke of Hamilton, with lineage traceable with labyrinthine luck back to the Plantagenant Kings. The tensions in this good lady's life were multiplied by her taking up with the new Methodist form of religion. On the one hand it was an emotional release for the unappeased sexual appetites of her widow-hood, but, on the other hand, the self-denial of Methodist discipline and distrust of leisure, is what she wished to impose on her son William. Her own politics approved its reverance for existing forms of Government and social institutions, but also its opposition to corruption and its criticism of the wealthy. Enough contradictions here to reconcile the most energetic of soul-searchers. Fonthill Splendens and its contents was created for amusement and therefore was the work of Satan. It was not hers to sell, however, it belonged to her son and the best she could do was endeavour to offset its influences by a tough tutorial regime, by destroying some of the Oriental prints which had fascinated the boy, and by following as closely as possible the Wesleyan code — "he that plays when a child will play when he is a man". In this she was also notably unsuccessful.

William's coming-of-age party in September 1781 followed an extensive Grand Tour through France and Italy, during which the main tendencies of his life had fixed themselves. His passions for collecting books and fine art, his writing and his fascination with all things oriental were confirmed.

The party at Fonthill was a proclamation of defiance; a signal of revolt against all future constraints; a lavish extravaganza that no other golden youth could attempt to better.

On the surrounding downs high bonfires were lit to spread the news in old beacon fashion and to form a glowing backdrop. In front of the house a great piazza was laid out on which stood an illuminated triumphal arch. On the lake, boats were got up and paraded to look like a Venetian Regatta. Musicians were hidden in the thickets and the ceremonial parade through the park to the Grecian Temple was climaxed with a huge display of fireworks and sound effects. Beckford himself was certainly responsible for many of the ideas. He adored theatrical effects and employed Philip de Loutherbourg, the dramatic painter who was winning acclaim in David Garrick's theatre for his ingenious stage effects and mechanical devices. In Sheridan's *The Critic*, first produced in 1779, he had an amazing climax showing the destruction of the Armada with the fleets engaging, music, battle effects, the sending in of fireships and a final montage of the most famous English rivers set to Handel's Water Music. We have no detailed account of de Loutherbourg's contribution to the Beckford party, but from hints in the correspondence it is possible that he brought with him his new Eidophusikon. This mechanical device which had had its first demonstration in February of that same year is now seen as one of the precursors of the cinema. The Eidophusikon was a large scale adult version of the popular childrens' peep-show, producing scenes and incidents "in progressive motion", accompanied by music and effects. Light effects were achieved by coloured glass and gauzes moving in front of the lamps. Painted cut-out settings and backdrops moved as scenes changed. The width of the stage was about six feet and the depth only eight feet, but the effect of distance possible by De Loutherbourg's skill in creating perspective was extraordinary. I saw a working model of this machine some years ago at a de Loutherbourg's exhibition with small spot-lights replacing the original oil lamps and a tape replacing the live musicians, but the theatrical magic was most convincing. One did indeed feel one was seeing for miles.

One of de Loutherbourg's most remarkable and significant

shows on the Eidophusikon which he perfected during 1781, was his "Satan arraying his Troops on the Bank of the Fiery Lake, with the raising of the Palace of Pandemonium", which included erupting volcanos and all kinds of fiery effects. Knowing the tastes and persuasiveness of Beckford, it is not stretching conjecture too far to suppose that the artist was cajolled into presenting this apocalyptic vision of Hell with its powerful central figure bringing forth fiery demons amidst thunder and lightning. It is an image, not only appealing to Beckford because of its inspiration in Milton's *Paradise Lost*, or its teasing reference to his own personal situation as a millionaire prince, but also because it has parallels in his beloved Arabian myths.

Friends and relations planned a great future for William; he would enter Parliament and soon petition for a peerage and the seat in the Lords which the family deserved; he would marry well, have sons to continue the dynasty and bring increased prestige, as well as power, to the family estates and businesses. Within five years all public ambitions were shattered by a series of scandals, misfortunes, betrayals which turned respectable society against Beckford and turned him into a suspicious recluse with little alternative but to use his considerable energies and talents to cultivate a private and eccentric world.

Almost all the cast of this tragedy were guests of Beckford's house-party in the old Fonthill house for Christmas 1781, the same year he officially came of age. They were his chosen companions for an experience of oriental sensuality. Each had a part to play in Beckford's doom. Amongst the guests were Louisa Beckford, her sisters, brother George Pitt with the notorious Sophia Musters, Samuel Henley with a group of boys, William Courtenay and Alexander Cozens. The atmosphere of the occasion is recalled by William Beckford in a note dated December 9th, 1838 and quoted in Oliver's biography from which these extracts are taken:

Immured we were "au pied de la lettre" for three days following — doors and windows so strictly closed that neither common day light nor common place visitors could get in or even peep in ... Our société was extremely youthful and lovely to look upon ... The solid Egyptian Hall looked as if hewn out of a living rock — the line of appartments and apparently endless passages extending from it either side were all vaulted — an interminable staircase, which when you looked down it — appeared as deep as the well in the pyramid — and when you looked up — was lost in vapour, led to suites of stately apartments gleaming with marble pavements — as polished as glass — and gaudy ceilings ... Through all these suites — through all these galleries — did we roam and wander — too often hand in hand — strains of music swelling forth at intervals ... Here nothing was dull or vapid ... all was essence — the slightest approach to sameness was here untolerated — monotony of every kind was banished. Even the uniform splendour of gilded roofs — was partially obscured by the vapour of wood aloes ascending in wreaths from cassolettes placed low on the silken carpets in porcelain salvers of the richest japan. The delirium of delight into which our young and fervid bosoms were cast by such a combination of seductive influences may be conceived but too easily. Even at this long, sad distance from those days and nights of exquisite refinements, chilled by age, still more by the coarse unpoetic tenor of the present disenchanting period — I still feel warmed and irradiated by the recollections of that strange, necromantic light which Loutherbourg had thrown over what absolutely appeared a realm of Fairy, or rather, perhaps, a Demon Temple deep beneath the earth set apart for tremendous mysteries — and yet how soft, how genial was this quiet light. Whilst the wretched world without lay dark, and bleak, and howling, whilst the storm was raging against our massive walls and the snow drifting in clouds, the very air of summer seemed playing around us — the choir of low-toned melodious voices continued to sooth our ear, and that every sense might in turn receive its blandishments, tables covered with delicious viands and fragrant flowers — glided forth, by the aid of mechanism at stated intervals, from the richly draped, and amply curtained recesses of the enchanted precincts. The glowing haze investing every object, the mystic look, the vastness, the intricacy of this vaulted labyrinth occasioned so bewildering an effect that it became impossible for any to define — at the moment — where he stood, where he had been, or to whether he was wandering — such was the confusion — the perplexity so many illuminated storys of infinitely varied apartments gave rise to. It was, in short, the realisation of romance in its most extravagent intensity. No wonder such scenery inspired the description of the Halls of Eblis.

It is tempting to see Alexander Cozens as a kind of Mephistopheles to Beckford's Faust, or as the Giaour, the hideous Indian messenger of Eblis; an oriental Satan character in Arabian folklore which Beckford was to use in "*Vathek*", his own grotesque and fantastic story of a journey to damnation in the Palace of Subterranean fire where Eblis rules. The Giaour is the purveyor of "singular curiosities", conjuror of visions, inflamer of troubled imaginations. Cozens has less magic, but is quite as insidious. Employed as drawing master to the adolescent Beckford, the Russian-born artist seems to have exerted a powerful influence on the boy. He was a clever teacher certainly "almost as full of systems as the Universe", wrote Beckford later, but while others, including Chatham, the boy's godfather and Lettice, his tutor, wished to discourage the growth of interest in oriental art of an escapist and often sadistic nature, he was doing the opposite. He actively encouraged the boy's passion for the exotic, intro-

duced him to the tales of Ossian and *The Arabian Nights* and
Eastern Fantasy until it was an unquenchable life-long force,
continuously threatening any realistic judgment or decision
about the real world. Beckford nicknamed him "The Persian".

He encouraged, how actively we can only guess at, the amoral
yearnings of the boy. Here was a very rich young man without
a father but destined perhaps for some high political or at least
social honour, and Cozens seems to have openly encouraged him
to pursue homosexual relationships in public at a time when
social conventions regarded them as criminal. He is himself the
recipient of an extraordinary series of incandescent letters from
Beckford which show what kind of grip he had on the young
correspondent's mind. A visit to Switzerland in 1777 to live
"en famille" and polish up his culture, accompanied by Cozens,
was cut short by his mother when she received disquieting
rumours about William's "gay" escapades.

William Courtenay was only eleven when Beckford stayed with
his father, Viscount Courtenay, at Powderham Castle in Devon
during a short English tour with his tutor Lettice in 1779. He fell
in love with the boy and began a complicated relationship with him.

At Christmas 1781, this beautiful child was thirteen, the model
for a flattering portrait in *Vathek*.

> Gulchenrouz could write in various characters and paint upon vellum
> the most elegant arabesques that fancy could devise. His sweet voice
> accompanied the lute in the most enchanting manner ... The verses he
> composed inspired that unresting languor, so frequently fatal to the
> female heart. The women all doated on him; and though he had passed
> his thirteenth year, they still detained him in the harem ...

But whether Beckford's passion was carnal and requited, or
fraternal and aesthetic made no difference in 1783, when he
was using his influence and wealth to apply for a peerage and seat
in the House of Lords. A mutual friend betrayed the affair —
homosexuality was still a criminal matter — and Beckford found
himself in the glare of a public scandal and his social ambitions
blocked. In order to avoid possible court proceedings and an even
bigger furore, he was hustled into voluntary but necessary exile;
forced to travel without destination until time healed the wound.
Although he was eventually able to return to England, he was
never again accepted by respectable English society and the chance
of a peerage never recurred.

Despite the foregoing, or because of it, who knows, Beckford
was attracted to older and experienced women, the kind of
well-born and unstuffy ladies who formed a kind of demi-monde

of high society. Lady Craven, later Margravine of Anspach, Countess Rosenberg, the friend of Casanova, Emma Hamilton of Nelson fame, were all in turn attracted to him. They flattered and amused him and led him astray; he found in their company intimacy without commitment, and encouragement for his sexual fantasies.

Louisa, wife of Peter Beckford, 18th century fox hunting authority, was more dangerous because she became seriously involved with William during the summer of 1781 while he was visiting and wanted to leave home and come after him, despite her husband and children he was her "loverly infernal". Yet that her attraction to William was not necessarily straightforward is clear from the fact that both she and William Courtenay are both at Fonthill for the Christmas house-party, sharing his attentions. Louisa, "as sprightly as an antelope, and full of wanton gaiety", is Nourinihar, daughter of the Emir in *Vathek*, inseparable from the boy Gulchenrouz (William Courtenay).

> Both had the same tastes and amusements; the same long, languishing looks; the same tresses; the same fair complexions, and when Gulchenrouz appeared in the dress of his cousin, he seemed more feminine than even herself.

To cut through this web, Beckford's mother proposed a practical dynastic marriage with Lady Margaret, daughter of the Fourth Earl of Aboyne, which was to serve the double purpose of killing scandal and preparing the ground for the peerage which the family's wealth demanded. The marriage was celebrated in May and the couple left the country for an extended visit to Italy.

Samuel Henley was another guest who later proved a bitter disappointment to Beckford. Henley had been a professor at the William and Mary College in Virginia and had returned to England and lucrative private tutoring, as he saw the American War going against the loyalists. He was an expert in old oriental literature and Beckford found him useful and interesting.

"Thoroughly imbued with all that passed at Fonthill during this voluptuous festival", Beckford rushed back to London and wrote *Vathek* in less than a week, and in French, a language in which he was completely fluent.

In May that year he went on another continental trip, this time a honeymoon to Italy with his young wife and left the translation to his old tutor, Lettice. This got bogged down because Lettice had not the scholarly knowledge of Arabic folklore to make a correct interpretation, so Henley was asked to step in. In the meantime, Beckford was working up four Episodes, extra tales which were to slot into the penultimate section of the book, and was writing to commend progress, discuss details of style and make it quite clear that on no account should the book be published without the new segment. In 1784 the Courtenay scandal broke, and Beckford was bundled off to Lausanne in July the following year, together with his wife and baby daughter. Before the Episodes were completed Beckford's wife died in childbirth, a great blow, leaving him without his moral lifebuoy and bitter and depressed. Then to cap it all he heard that Henley had published *Vathek* in England without acknowledging his authorship, and suggesting that his adaptation was from an Arabic original. Beckford's disappointment and confusion was magnified by the distance of his place of exile, and whereas the proper authorship was eventually established, any hope of immediate credit or benefit was shattered.

Vathek went on to have a certain success and considerable influence amongst the Romantic poets and writers, Byron in particular, but the episode with Henley left such a bad taste that it effectively discouraged future work. Beckford turned increasingly to collecting rare books and works of art, to gardening and to building, all of which he was able to indulge in with the fortune at his disposal.

Beckford willingly received the income from his Jamaican plantations but he could not be persuaded to get personally concerned in their management and he never visited Jamaica, although on one occasion he got as far as setting sail. The Alderman had not left a tidy situation to his inheritors. There were outstanding loans to planters, secured by mortgages on estates, there were arrangements on commissions of goods, there were a number of leases whose terms were in dispute, there were problems concerning the actual management and productivity of the Beckford plantations. There were the conflicting claims of relatives and the natural children of the Alderman.

At every turn there were opportunities for fraud, concealment of income, denial of contracts — a whole gamut of deceit once the strong hand of the Alderman was removed. Banished from England over his alleged relationship with William Courtenay, travelling in Europe, there was no reason why he should not use some of the time on a West Indies visit. In 1787 special arrangements were made to enable Beckford to land at Falmouth without the law intervening, so that he could rendezvous with the *Julius Caesar*, one of the family's own ships — "No one embarked for transportation with a heavier heart", he wrote, but the leg of the journey to Lisbon was more than enough, and he disembarked in Portugal, where he decided to stay for the time being in luxury and seclusion. The realities of running a business empire appalled him, like his hero The Caliph Vathek, "he did not think ... that it was necessary to make a hell of this world to enjoy paradise in the next". A good market for sugar meant one thing to Beckford — money to pursue his enthusiasm for collecting and building. Writing to Lady Craven in January 1790 he said "One of my new estates in Jamaica brought me home seven thousand pounds last year more than usual. So I am growing rich, and mean to build towers, and sing hymns to the powers of heaven on their summits"...

> when the workmen had raised their structure a cubit in the day time, two cubits more were added in the night. The expedition, with which the fabric arose, was not a little flattering to the vanity of Vathek: he fancied, that even insensible matter shewed a forwardness to subserve his designs ...
>
> His pride arrived at its height, when having ascended, for the first time, the fifteen hundred stairs of his tower, he cast his eyes below, and beheld men not larger than pismires: mountains than shells; and cities, than beehives. The idea, which such an elevation inspired of his own grandeur, completely bewildered him: he was almost ready to adore himself; till lifting his eyes upward, he saw the stars as high above him as they appeared when he stood on the surface of the earth. He consoled himself, however, for this intruding and unwelcome perception of his littleness, with the thought of being great in the eyes of others; and flattered himself that the light of his mind would extend beyond the reach of his sight, and extort from the stars the decrees of his destiny.
>
> (Vathek — William Beckford)

Like Elizabeth Taylor's diamonds or William Hearst's Xanadu mansion, Beckford's Fonthill Abbey was a symbol of conspicuous consumption on such a scale that it became a legend in its own time and has continued to stir the romantic imagination ever since.

Towers were an obsession of Beckford's even as a teenager. A yearning to be able to retire, like the oriental potentates of his favourite Arabic and Chinese pictures and tales, to the seclusion of luxurious towers appears again and again in early letters and writings. As the real world disgusted or deserted him, the attraction of towers, real or imaginary, increased. He bought pictures, often below his own high standards of taste, where towers were featured, and dealers exploited his weakness.

Portugal, where he had jumped ship on the way to Jamaica, provided a further inspiration. Here he had stayed in a luxurious and atmospheric monastery whose grandiose site, theatrical architecture and seclusion particularly appealed to him. But even here, as the war clouds gathered once again all over Europe, he could not find a permanent haven. At home in England Beckford's family and friends had secured an understanding with the Government on the Courtenay business which meant Beckford could return home, but he had never liked his father's house, too solid and on too low and damp a site to please. From this, the idea of a large ruin, complete with tower and habitable quarters on a suitably dramatic site within the Fonthill estate took firm root. The obvious man for the job was James Wyatt, whose output of mansions, castles, abbeys and assorted ruins across the country was already prodigious. He was also engaged in restoration of Gothic cathedrals and was working on Salisbury Cathedral from 1789 onwards.

Between Wyatt and his patron the project grew from a glorified summer-house to a full-blooded Gothic inspired abbey on a vast scale. Both men were megalomaniacs and both were impatient. The result as we know was both glorious and fatally flawed.

First of all the setting was extraordinary. Even before any architect had been approached, Beckford contracted for a wall twelve foot high with cheveux de frise, about seven miles long to encircle an area of some 500 acres of his estate, the only entrances to which were guarded gates. He called this the "monastic demesne" and allowed the park to grow wild, but also began a huge programme of planting to make the place even more romantic. The site for the abbey was a commanding one with extensive views. One of the Turner sketchbooks, preserved in the British Museum dated 1799, is devoted to Fonthill Abbey. Turner, the rising young topographer and water-colourist, was summoned by Beckford and spent three weeks making numerous sketches of the unfinished tower and other structures from varying distances and in different lights. Some of the drawings are rich in architectural detail and show the Tower only just built in a timber skeleton, protruding above a level of about 150 feet, whereas the wash drawings done from a distance have projected the tower to its full height, but wisely avoid detail. From these, Turner made a short series of "bespoke" watercolours which were sold to Beckford for 35 guineas each.

Some of these were shown in the following year's Royal Academy Exhibition, in those days the most important artistic event of the year. Those not already in the know could not have failed to be made curious by the ghostly and rather vague romantic Turner images, and their preservation has helped preserve something of the mystery and fascination of Fonthill Abbey for posterity.

Xanadu on a Wiltshire Hilltop

The visit to Fonthill was useful to Turner in other ways. Two large and important Claude landscapes which had belonged to the Altieri family in Italy had been smuggled out of Naples with the help of the Navy and had been bought by Beckford to put in his new planned galleries in the Abbey. In the meantime, they hung in the old house at Fonthill and Turner was able to study them in detail and at leisure. One has to remember that there were as yet no national collections of painting on public view in England, and the only opportunity for an artist to study important paintings was in the private houses of the gentry. Claude was a seminal influence on Turner's later work. In addition, Beckford became a major Turner patron by his purchase of a large Turner painting called *The Fifth Plague of Egypt.*

Artists, builders and artisans were almost the only visitors to Fonthill. The Grand Babel as Beckford called it, required huge quantities of specially commissioned stained glass, fabrics and furnishings. As the building grew, so did Beckford's impatience. His sense of humour about it remained — "some people drink to forget their unhappiness; I do not drink, I build", he said, but the need for self-dramatisation became uncontrollable. At first the pace of building was closely geared to the profits of good sugar years, but gradually caution was abandoned and the work was done on credit. Only the ambitious scheme for the Eastern Transept was made to wait until the summer of 1812 when the price of sugar shot up in the expectation of peace in Europe and the re-opening of European markets.

But the Abbey was far from complete when Beckford planned a grand party and reception for Lord Nelson and Emma Hamilton at Christmas 1800, a party to honour the victor of the Battle of the Nile and conqueror of the Mediterranean, and to demonstrate Beckford's munificence and mastery of the grandiose theatrical event. So the pace of building was accelerated and another legend born, that of the imperious command of this Caliph of Fonthill who could command building projects up and down the country to be halted, while every available building worker was drawn to Fonthill to labour by day and by night by the light of hundreds of flaring torches to get the job complete for the big visit. Beckford, like a mad scientist, stands amidst it all shouting encouragement as buckets of plaster and materials fly hither and thither.

Enough of the Abbey was completed in time for the festivities. Britton, who was writing not long after the event, described the occasion.

he had concentrated within his own walls, the most delightful blandishments of art, the fascinations of talent, and the choicest luxuries for the palate; besides the most rare and most delicious viands, fruits and wines, with oderiferous plants, flowers, and essences, some of the first vocal and instrumental performers were engaged, a military band was provided and Fonthill volunteers were prepared and disciplined.

Nelson and Emma were met at Salisbury by civic dignitaries and a military band which led the coach towards Fonthill, crowds cheering them on their way. It was all very flattering to Nelson's ego — after all he was in his own, and in the popular mind, "a man of destiny, an agent of great purposes".

The festivities at Fonthill lasted several days.

The abbey or monastic fete on the evening of the 23rd was the most remarkable period of the gala. A procession of carriages, horses, soldiers, moved from the old house to the abbey in the evening. Flambeaux, torches and many thousand lamps were distributed on the sides of the road among the woods; whilst bands of music and files of soldiers were stationed in different places to greet and charm the company as they passed. Everything, indeed, was provided to steal upon the senses, to dazzle the eye, and to bewilder the fancy. After passing through a long, winding umbrageous avenue — after hearing the sounds of distant, near, and varied instruments, with their reverberations among the woods and dells, and contemplating the vivid and solemn effects of bright flitting lights and deep shadows, the company was conducted to the abbey . . .

The guests arrived at the grand entrance with its huge thirty foot high doors, studded with nails. Above them loomed the huge octagonal tower. Mysterious hooded figures with large wax torches lit the way up to the grand staircase while dark shadows flickered in the vaulted ceiling eighty feet above. At the top of the stairs the guests found themselves in an octagonal room whose roof was an awe-inspiring 128 feet above them. They were then led into "the great saloon", the Cardinal's parlour, furnished with rich tapestries, long curtains of purple damask, ebony tables and chairs studded with ivory, of various but antique form, "where they were led to a 50 foot long refectory table and served a magnificent dinner from a long line of silver dishes. Afterwards they were guided through other rooms and galleries, equally luxurious, to a salon for a theatrical performance in which the flattering high point was Lady Hamilton in the role of Agrippina, bearing the ashes of Germanicus in a golden urn and presenting herself to the Roman people with the design of exciting them to revenge the death of her husband. After this moving piece, the assembled company returned to the old mansion house for supper and rest.

In 1807, after more building, Beckford moved into the Abbey and sold Fonthill Splendens, a house which had reputedly cost his father £150,000 to rebuild after the fire of 1755, to a demolition firm for £9,000. Many of the paintings and other works of art which did not fit into the new setting were sold in public auctions and even more new items bought for the Abbey. In this dramatic but extraordinarily inconvenient house Beckford lived with few companions, collecting, writing letters, composing some short literary pieces, posting up to London to visit the theatre.

In 1822, when the bottom had fallen out of the sugar market and the Beckford businesses were in serious trouble he was forced to sell Fonthill Abbey and got a price which enabled him to pay off all his debts and leave him a very large capital sum with which to start again.

After he had done so, a builder on his death-bed, confessed that the foundations of the Tower which had been specified and paid for, had not been built, and the Tower was dangerous. The new owner was told immediately and replied that it would probably last his lifetime. Nevertheless, it collapsed in 1825 and the Abbey crumbled into Gothic ruins.

In the last twenty years of his life, Beckford moved to Bath where he built another, but less flamboyant tower, and gathered together a collection of books and pictures no less splendid than before. He died in 1844 at the age of 84.

Extravagance is the middle name of most West Indian planters in the 18th century, but none spent money so fast and so ostentatiously as William Beckford II. His huge parties, staged like grand opera, his purchase of rare books and pictures, and above all, the building of Fonthill cost hundreds of thousands of pounds in the money of the period, which makes it millions today. The main source of this money was the sugar grown on the Beckford plantations in Jamaica, with the labour and lives of thousands of slaves. Beckford left no sons, his great collection of art was sold or dispersed, Fonthill Abbey had fallen down long before his death and the family businesses were run down or sold. Hazlitt, the great essayist and contemporary of Beckford wrote of Fonthill:

> It is a desert of magnificence, a glittering waste of laborious idleness, a cathedral turned into a toy shop, an immense museum of all that is most curious and costly, and at the same time, most worthless, in the productions of art and nature.

Examining the catalogues of the sales of Fonthill treasures, it is quite clear that Beckford was an astute and powerful patron, commissioning works from then contemporary artists like Turner when it was helpful to them, as well as buying wisely from the past. The association of Beckford with James Wyatt produced Fonthill Abbey, one of the most important buildings and images of the Gothic Revival. Kenneth Clark calls it "that wonderful building (which) concentrated in itself all the Romanticism of the 1790's and was the epitome of 18th century Gothic". Beckford's writing attracted the praise of much greater contemporaries like Byron and Shelley and later poets such as Swinburne and Mallarmé. It is impossible to write off such a man, but it is also unlikely, given his circumstances and character, that he could ever have fitted the image of a great politician or man of affairs that his over-ambitious mother and godfather Chatham wished for him.

Postscript

The independent Caribbean Commonwealth countries, formerly British colonies, bear their history like a festering sore. Their past associations with slavery are still a bitter memory and even today in a free society which is their own, workers may refuse to cut cane; the ghosts of those gentlemen of fortune — the absentee bosses of yesterday, are still around.

Jamaica, Barbados, the Windward and Leeward Islands, Trinidad and Tobago and British Guiana, are the unnatural products of man-made society whose only objective was to "rap and rend" as much sugar from the soil as quickly and as profitably as possible and to keep possible competitors out of the game. These islands came to be populated by a massive and forced migration of the peoples of West Africa across the Atlantic totalling some 15 million over the whole period of slavery together with a much smaller number of Europeans, lured, kidnapped or transported during the 17th century religous and political persecutions. The roots of these people were systematically smashed in the cruel and artifical living conditions of forced labour on the plantations.

To the British Government, to the merchants in the Cities of London, Bristol, Liverpool and other centres of trade, to the officers of the Army and the Navy making their reputations and fortunes in the cannon's mouth of profitable commercial war, the colonies were simply tropical gardens to be cropped for the exclusive benefit of the mother-country. When their purpose was served, the juice squeezed out, they were simple to abandon.

The Emancipation of British slaves, which was celebrated in 1834 as a great humanitarian act of a great civlizing nation, could also be viewed more cynically as a gloss stemming from the surge

127

of evangelical piety which Victorian society affected to cover up its own particular hypocricies, and forms of economic malpractice. Slavery was part of an economic system, which it must be evident to all, was no longer profitable to the mother-country and was now a positive obstacle to free trade and the achievement of new and grandiose imperial schemes elsewhere in the world. The planters and their interests had become embarassing anachronisms to the exuberant machine-minded leaders of the new industrial age which was dawning in Britain. The cost of sugar production by the old plantation method of hand and hoe and the use of primitive Renaissance engines, was now higher than the price finished sugar fetched in the market-place. "No one" ranted Lord Redesdale in 1826, "would advance a shilling on British West India property." The volume of British manufactured goods shipped to the Caribbean fell dramatically. These old "members of the body politic", "the nursery of British seamen", the root of "the pleasure, glory and grandeur of England," "this great circle of trade and navigation", and so on and so forth, all the extravagant phrases of the mercantilist spokesmen are reduced to one short phrase in the new jargon of the time — a Dead Letter! What was more, the British demand for sugar at home to satisfy the cake-eating and tea-swilling public far outstripped the annual output of the whole West Indies, while cheaper, better sugar was pressing in from the East if only the artificial wall of preferential pricing built to protect the British planter against the "filthy foreigner" could be pulled down. The hour was certainly at hand.

When the hour of liberation came, there were some 668,000 slaves to be freed. An elaborate charade of apprenticeships was created to hold slaves on the plantation many further years, and £20,000,000 had been voted by Parliament as a free gift to the planters in compensation for their loss. Most of this in fact went to pay off mortgages and other debts of planters with merchants and agents in London. The money did very little to prop up the reeling economy of the islands but gave the factors and bankers an unexpected bonus with which to invest in the financial or industrial development of Victorian Britain.

Those planters who freed themselves from debt and tried to struggle on, found themselves in conditions of economic decline and political confusion. And far from being the centre of a great humanitarian rehabilitation programme conducted with all the panoply of 19th century philanthropy, the former slave population was completely neglected. For the mother country and its leaders, interest was elsewhere. The Caribbean colonies were allowed to shrivel away to economic nothingness, Lloyd George's "slums of the British Empire."

And while the poverty and the unemployment and the overcrowding continued, the ex-slaves also continued to be exploited. The process did not stop throughout the colonial 19th century and right up to independence. Countless reports speak of it and nothing gets done. To take only one instance, during the bitter economic riots in the Trinidadian oilfields in 1937, the Secretary of the Colony wrote . . . "an industry has no right to pay dividends at all until it pays a fair wage to labour and gives the labourer decent conditions". At the time, the oil companies were declaring dividends of 35% and more. Similar things were happening elsewhere.

If we believe in our heart of hearts, that we are somehow more compassionate and alert to social injustice in this more enlightened epoch with its concern for human rights, and that we could not nowadays allow or connive in silence to the sort of examples of man's inhumanity to man which form the backdrop of this book, let us look again. Plantation slavery in its old form may not exist but the poor and the weak can be led down other sorts of paths.

For years in Sri Lanka (formerly Ceylon) the teapickers on the Brooke Bond estates have been held to starvation wages, and only independent medical testimony revealed the appalling mortality amongst young children and its relationship to the degraded way of life which villagers were forced to lead. And what about those enlightened British companies who intoned a public prayer against Apartheid in South Africa, while paying the coloured and black workers in their subsidiaries there an even lower wage than the national norm. Business is only business we are continually told. Now we have the dossier in *The Guardian* newspaper in April this year about the extensive exploitation of child labour in Hong Kong by large and famous companies producing for the British toy, clothes and electronics markets. A hospital report of children under eleven badly injured by machines; sweated and cramped workshops which Charles Dickens and Lord Shaftesbury would have recognised; piece rates which are an insult to human dignity. Why? because poverty and overcrowding create the desperate conditions where almost anything is better than nothing, and where no restrictive laws operate it is possible for shrewd companies to exploit the situation, especially where administrators and judges in a British Crown Colony are prepared to condone it.

Independance in the Caribbean Islands brought no easy solutions. Even were all the many islands parts of one economy, the total population would be under 4 million and with few natural resources, that's a small economy. But in fact each island prefers to function in isolation which is another legacy of the commercial rivalry generated in colonial days. So little Montserrat has only 13,000 inhabitants and Anguilla far less. Barbados has almost a quarter of a million on a space as small as the Isle of Wight. Few of the islands can depend on any industry other than agriculture and have to export to survive. This means bananas, cotton, and sugar. Sugar is a noose that such ricketty agricultural economies cannot slip even now and one of the bitter ironies is that with such appalling overcrowding and endemic unemployment it has never been possible to modernize with labour-saving machinery. The whip has gone but it is still essentially the old method of cultivation. Is it any wonder there are bad memories? Is it any wonder that emigration remains a lasting hope and ambition for so many West Indians? Is it any wonder that the word Planter has come to mean all that is unforgivable in our Colonial past.

Bibliography

Bibliography
RAGATZ, L. J., *Guide to the Study of British Caribbean History 1763-1864*, (Washington D.C.), 1930.

Documentary Material
Calendar of State Papers. Colonial Series. America and West Indies 1574-1733, (London), 1862-1939.
DONNAN, E., (ed.) *Documents Illustrative of the History of the Slave Trade to America*, Vol. I and II.
Hakluyt Society. *Colonising Expeditions to the West Indies and Guiana 1623-1667*, 2nd Series No. LVI, 1925, (ed.) Harlow, V. T.
The Original Writings and Correspondence of Richard Hakluyt, 2nd Series No. LXXVI-LXXVII, 1935
Journal of the Commissioners for Trade and Plantations 1704-1782, (London), 1920-1938.
Slave Holding Compensation Accounts, The, 1838.

Histories
EDWARDS, Bryan, *History of British Colonies in the West Indies, 1793.*
LIGON, R., *History of Barbados*, 1657.
LONG, Edward, *History of Jamaica*, 3 vols., (London), 1774.
SCHOMBURGK, Sir R., *History of Barbados*, 1848.

Old Printed Works
BECKFORD, Peter, *Thoughts on Hunting.*
BECKFORD, William, *A Descriptive Account of the Island of Jamaica*, 1790.
BOURNE, *Famous London Merchants*, 1868.
BRITTON, D., *Graphic and Literary Illustrations of Fonthill Abbey*, 1823.
DALBY, Thomas, Sir, *An Historical Account of the Rise and Growth of the West India Colonies*, (London), 1690.
DAVIS, N. D., *Cavaliers and Roundheads of Barbados 1650-1652*, 1887.
LEWIS, M. G., *Journal of a West India Proprietor*, (London), 1834.
LITTLETON, E., *The Groans of the Plantations*, (London), 1689.
Liverpool Guide, The, 1796.
MACGRATH, (ed.), *Bristol in the Eighteenth Century*, (David & Charles), 1972.
MADDEN, R. R., *A Twelve Months' Residence in the West Indies*, (London), 1834.
POSTLETHWAYT, M., *The Universal Dictionary of Trade and Commerce*, 1751.
PURCELL, E. S., *Life of Cardinal Manning*, 1896.
WENTWORTH, Trelawney, *The West India Sketchbook*, 2 vols., 1834.
YOUNG, William, *The West India Commonplace Book*, 1807.

Modern Secondary Sources
ALEXANDER, Boyd, *England's Wealthiest Son*, 1962.
ANDREWS, *Essays in Colonial History*, 1931.

Bibliography

BENNETT, J. H., *Bondsmen and Bishops*, (Berkeley, California), 1958.
BLUNT, R., *Mrs Montagu. Her Letters and Friendships*, 2 Vols., 1923.
BOLTON, A. T., *The Architecture of Robert and James Adam*, 1922.
BROCKMAN, H. A. N., *The Caliph of Fonthill*, 1956.
BROODBANK, J. G., *History of the Port of London*, 1921.
BURN, W. L., *The British West Indies*, (London), 1951.
Cambridge History of the British Empire, Vol. I to 1783, (Cambridge University Press), 1928.
CRATON and WALVIN, *A Jamaican Plantation. Worthy Park.*
CUNDALL, F., *Historic Jamaica*, (Institute of Jamaica), 1915.
DODD, A. H., *The Industrial Revolution in North Wales*, (Cardiff), 1933.
DUNN, R. S., *Sugar and Slaves*, (Cape), 1973.
GILL, C., *Merchants and Mariners of the Eighteenth Century*, (London), 1961.
HAMILTON, H., *An Economic History of Scotland in the Eighteenth Century.*
HARLOW, V. T., *Christopher Codrington 1688-1710*, (Oxford University Press), 1928.
HARLOW, V. T., *A History of Barbados 1625-1685*, (Oxford University Press), 1926.
HOBSBAWM, E., *Industry and Empire*, (Penguin), 1968.
HOWARD, R. M., (ed.), *Records and Letters of the Family of the Longs of Longville, Jamaica and Hampton Lodge*, 1925.
LILLYWHITE, B., *London Coffee Houses*, (London), 1963.
LLOYD, C., *The Navy and the Slave Trade*, (London), 1949.
LOWE, R., *The Codrington Correspondence 1743-1851*, (London), 1951.
MACINNES, C. M., *England's Slavery*, (Bristol), 1934.
MACKENZIE-GRIEVE, A., *Last Years of the English Slave Trade in Liverpool 1750-1807*, (F. Cass), 1968.
MATHIESON, W. L., *British Slavery and Its Abolition 1823-1838*, (London), 1926.
NAMIER, Lewis, *Crossroads of Power*, (London), 1962.
NAMIER, Lewis, *Structure of Politics at the Accession of George III*, 1957.
NAMIER, Lewis, *England in the Age of the American Revolution*, (London), 1961.
NICOLE, C., *The West Indies*, (Hutchinson), 1966.
PARES, R., *War and Trade in the West Indies 1739-1763*, (Oxford University Press), 1936.
PARES, R., *A Historian's Business (Essays)*, (Oxford), 1961.
PARES, R., *Essays Presented to Sir Lewis Namier.*
PARES, R., *A West India Fortune*, (London), 1950.
PATTERSON, O., *Sociology of Slavery*, (London), 1967.
PENSON, L. M., *The Colonial Agents of the British West Indies*, (London), 1924.
PITMAN, F. W., *The Development of the British West Indies 1700-1763*, (New Haven), 1917.
POPE-HENNESY, James, *The Sins of the Father*, (London), 1967.
RAGATZ, L. G., *The Fall of the Planter Class in the British Caribbean 1763-1833*, (New York), 1928.
RUDÉ, G., *Hanoverian London 1714-1808*, (London), 1971.
SUMMERSON, J., *Georgian London*, (Penguin), 1973.
WADSWORTH, and MANN, *The Cotton Trade and Industrial Lancashire*, (Manchester), 1931.
WARNER, A., *Sir Thomas Warner; Pioneer of the West Indies*, (London), 1933.
WILLIAMS, E., *Capitalism and Slavery*, (London), 1964.
WILLIAMSON, J. A., *A Short History of British Expansion*, 1933.
WILLIAMSON, J. A., *The Caribee Islands Under Proprietary Patents*, 1921.
WILSON, C., *England's Apprenticeship 1603-1763*, 1965.
YORKE, Philip, (ed.), *The Diary of John Baker 1751-1778*, (London), 1931.

Index